Jonathan Larkin

Paradise Bound

D0769647

Methuen Drama

Published by Methuen 2006

1 3 5 7 9 10 8 6 4 2

First published in 2006 by
Methuen Publishing Limited
11–12 Buckingham Gate
London SW1E 6LB

Methuen Publishing Limited Reg. No. 3543167

A CIP catalogue record for this book is available from
the British Library

ISBN 10: 0 413 77603 4
ISBN 13: 978 0 413 77603 7

Typeset by Country Setting, Kingsdown, Kent
Printed and bound in Great Britain by
Bookmarque Ltd, Croydon, Surrey

LIVERPOOL EVERYMAN AND PLAYHOUSE PRESENT
THE WORLD PREMIÈRE OF

PARADISE BOUND

BY JONATHAN LARKIN

LIVERPOOL EVERYMAN AND PLAYHOUSE

About the Theatres

In 2000, two great regional reps were merged into a single company. At the beginning of 2004, buoyed up by Liverpool's impending status as European Capital of Culture in 2008, they entered a new and dynamic era. By returning to producing on a major scale, the Everyman and Playhouse have reclaimed their place on the national stage and generated an energy that has attracted acclaim, awards and audience loyalty.

The Liverpool Everyman and Playhouse theatres are always looking to bring the people of Merseyside a rich and varied portrait of the theatrical landscape. We have a strong and passionate commitment to new writing. Today's playwrights are tomorrow's theatrical legacy.

There are few things more exciting in the life of a theatre than launching the first play of a young, local writer. Jonathan Larkin began his relationship with these theatres as part of our young writers group and is now one of our writers in residence thanks to The Henry Cotton Memorial Fund. *Paradise Bound* was given a reading last year in Everyword, our annual festival of new writing. It was clear then that it deserved a full production; full of warmth and humour it asked some tough questions of its community and indeed this city. Like many a great Liverpool writer before him, Jonathan Larkin writes with an equal measure of heart and acerbic wit about the city and the people that nurtured him.

Liverpool Everyman and Playhouse would like to thank all our current supporters:

Corporate Members A C Robinson and Associates, Benson Signs, Brabners Chaffe Street, c3 Imaging, Chadwick Chartered Accountants, Downtown Liverpool in Business, Duncan Sheard Glass, DWF Solicitors, EEF NorthWest, Grant Thornton, Hope Street Hotel, John Lewis, Mando Group, Morgenrot Chevaliers, Non Conform Design, Nviron Ltd, Synergy Colour Printing, The Mersey Partnership Victor Huglin Carpets

Trusts & Grant-Making Bodies
BBC Northern Exposure, BBC Radio Merseyside, The Eleanor Rathbone Charitable Trust, Five, The Harry Pilkington Trust, The Golsoncott Foundation,The Granada Foundation, Liverpool Culture Company, The Lynn Foundation, PH Holt Charitable Trust,The Pilkington General Fund, The Rex Makin Charitable Trust.

This theatre has the support of the Pearson Playwrights' Scheme sponsored by Pearson plc. Assisted by Business in the Arts: North West

Individual Supporters Peter and Geraldine Bounds, George C Carver, Councillor Eddie Clein, Mr and Mrs Dan Hugo, A Thomas Jackson, Ms D Leach, Frank D Paterson, Les Read, Sheena Streather, Frank D Thompson, DB Williams and all those who prefer to remain anonymous.

Liverpool Everyman and Playhouse is a registered charity no. 1081229
www.everymanplayhouse.com

NEW WRITING AT THE LIVERPOOL EVERYMAN AND PLAYHOUSE

"A remarkable renaissance"
(Liverpool Daily Post)

As well as a major expansion in production the Theatres' revival is driven by a passionate commitment to new writing. *Paradise Bound* is the latest in a rich and varied slate of world, European or regional premières which has been enthusiastically received by Merseyside audiences and helped to put Liverpool's theatre back on the national map.

"Lyrical, muscular, full of indignation and compassion"
(The Sunday Times on *Yellowman*)

Highly acclaimed productions have included the European première of *Yellowman* by Dael Orlandersmith which transferred to Hampstead Theatre and successfully toured nationally, and regional premières of Conor McPherson's *Port Authority* and Simon Block's *Chimps*. And in just over two years, the theatres will have produced seven world premières -*Fly* by Katie Douglas; *The Kindness of Strangers* by Tony Green; *Urban Legend* by Laurence Wilson; *The Morris* by Helen Blakeman; Gregory Burke's *On Tour* - (a co-production with London's Royal Court); *Unprotected* by Esther Wilson, John Fay, Tony Green, Lizzie Nunnery and *Paradise Bound* by Jonathan Larkin.

"The Everyman could wish for no finer 40th anniversary present than a return to form"
(The Guardian on *The Kindness of Strangers*)

Around the main production programme, the theatres run a range of projects and activities to create opportunities and offer support to writers at every career stage.

The commissioning programme invests in the creation of new work for both the Everyman and the Playhouse stages.

The Henry Cotton Writers on Attachment scheme is providing three young Liverpool writers with an intensive programme of creative and career development. Thanks to Five and to Pearson TV both Laurence Wilson and Tony Green recently benefited from year-long residencies. And an annual new writing festival, *Everyword*, offers a busy and popular week of seminars, sofa talks and work-in-progress readings.

"Laurence Wilson is another name to add to the theatre's long and glorious reputation for nurturing new talent"
(Liverpool Echo on *Urban Legend*)

The full programme at the Everyman and Playhouse blends this new work with bold interpretations of classic drama, and mixes our own 'Made in Liverpool' productions with carefully hand-picked touring shows. By doing so, we aim to offer the people of Merseyside a rich and satisfying theatrical diet. But if we are driven by one thing more than all others, it is the conviction that an investment in new writing is an investment in our theatrical future.

For more information about the Everyman and Playhouse - including the full programme, off-stage activities such as playwright support, and ways in which you can support our investment in talent - visit www.everymanplayhouse.com

CREDITS

THE CAST (IN ALPHABETICAL ORDER)

Ciaran Griffiths
Anthony

Kerry Peers
Ann

Mary Jo Randle
Kathleen

Michael Ryan
Danny

THE COMPANY

Writer	Jonathan Larkin
Director	Sue Dunderdale
Designer	Bob Bailey
Lighting Designer	Tina MacHugh
Sound Designer	Sean Pritchard
Costume Supervisor	Brian D Hanlon
Assistant Director	Adam Maher
Casting Director	Leila Bertrand
Production Manager	Emma Wright
Stage Manager	Natalia Cortes
Deputy Stage Manager	Lorraine Cheesmur
Assistant Stage Manager	Gary James
Lighting Operator	Breandan Ansdell
Stage Crew	Lindsey Bell
	Paul McDonough
Set Construction	Splinter
Dramaturg	Suzanne Bell

CAST

CIARAN GRIFFITHS
ANTHONY

Ciaran's television credits include:
The Street, Blue Murder, Gilmayo, Vincent, The Bill, Clocking Off, Emmerdale, Heartbeat Christmas Special, Stig Of The Dump, Where The Heart Is, Coronation Street, The Cop series II, *Always And Everyone, City Central* and *Knight's School.*

Film credits include:
There's Only One Jimmy Grimble.

KERRY PEERS
ANN

Kerry has worked extensively in theatre and television. She is best known for her roles as WDC Suzi Croft in *The Bill* and Helen Carey in *Brookside.*

Recent television credits include:
Casualty at Holby City Christmas Special.

Kerry's recent theatre credits include:
Billy Liar (Liverpool Playhouse); Blanche in *A Streetcar Named Desire* and Nurse Ratched in *One Flew Over The Cuckoo's Nest* (Clwyd Theatr Cymru); Matron in *Be My Baby*, Aunt Blanche in *Brighton Beach Memoirs* - for which she received the Manchester Evening News Award for Best Supporting Actress - and Anna in *The Government Inspector* (Oldham Coliseum).

Other theatre includes work for the RSC, the RNT and Scarborough.

CAST

MARY JO RANDLE
KATHLEEN

Mary Jo trained at RADA, where
she won the Bancroft Gold Medal.

Theatre credits include:
What's In The Cat? (Contact Theatre,
Manchester and Royal Court Upstairs);
Question Time (Arcola Theatre);
The Memory Of Water (Hampstead
Theatre); *Divine Right* (Birmingham
Repertory Theatre); *Revello* (Soho
Theatre); *Phaedra* (Lyric Hammersmith);
Les Liasons Dangereuses, *Philistines*,
As You Like It and *Troilus* and *Cressida*
(Royal Shakespeare Company)
and *Dearly Beloved* - a one woman
show (The Other Place, Stratford
and The Almeida Theatre)..

Television credits include: *Midsomer
Murders*, *Baby War*, *Olly's Prison*,
Between The Sheets, *Gifted*,
Cambridge Spies, *Cutting It*, *Victoria
Wood As Seen On TV*, *Inspector
Morse*, *The Lakes* I and II,
Born To Run and *The Bill*.

Film credits include:
Pierrepoint and *Bad Behaviour*.

MICHAEL RYAN
DANNY

Michael's theatre credits include:
The Doll Tower and *The Trial* (Unity
Theatre, Liverpool); *Play Your Cards
Right* (Various London Theatres);
Pause For Thought (Mermaid
Theatre, London); *Road* and
Hay Fever (Neptune Theatre,
Liverpool); Liz Lockhead's *Dracula*
(Everyman Theatre, Liverpool) and
The Longest Night Alone (Green
House/Philharmonic Hall, Liverpool).

Television credits include:
Dream Team, *Dockers* and
Innocent Party.

Film credits include: *Revengers
Tragedy*, *In His Life* (John Lennon
biopic) and *Across The Universe*.

COMPANY

JONATHAN LARKIN
WRITER

Jonathan is a Liverpool based writer. *Paradise Bound* is his first play.

Paradise Bound was originally developed through the Liverpool Everyman and Playhouse Young Writers' Programme, and an earlier draft of the play was performed, under the title *Master of None*, in a rehearsed reading during the theatres' Everyword new writing festival in 2004. Scenes from the play were also performed at the Queer Up North Festival (Contact Theatre, Manchester) where the audience voted for it as Best Play.

Jonathan is one of the Liverpool Everyman and Playhouse Henry Cotton Writers on Attachment for 2005/06. His second play, *Loose Lips*, is currently in development and will receive a rehearsed reading in this year's Everyword Festival.

For radio, Jonathan's credits include *Lost In Liverpool* (BBC Radio 3).

SUE DUNDERDALE
DIRECTOR

Recent theatre credits include:
Mrs Pat (York Theatre Royal); *Bottle Universe* (The Bush Theatre); *Cold Hands* (Theatre 503, Battersea); *Squint* (The Chelsea Theatre); *Too Clever By Half* (Rose Bruford Collage); *Killing the Cat* (Royal Court Theatre); *The House of Yes* (Soho Theatre Company); *Teendreams* (Guildhall Scholl of Drama); *Deborah's Daughter* (Library Theatre, Manchester); *The Land of the Living* (Royal Court Upstairs); *The Water Children* (National Theatre Studio).

Television credits include:
Eastenders, *Nativity Blues*, *Brookside*, *Coronation Street*, *Emmerdale*, *Casualty*, *The Bill*, *Heartbeat*, *Space Island One*, *The Blood That's In You*, *London Bridge*, *Justice*, *Rockface* and *A Fairytale Funeral*.

Sue has also written for film and television, and is currently Head of Directing at RADA.

BOB BAILEY
DESIGNER

In 2006 Bob will be the Set and Costume Designer for the UK tour of *The New Statesman* and for the forthcoming productions of *Manon Lescaut* and *Fedora*, (Opera Holland Park).

Theatre Credits include: *Falstaff* (Guildhall Opera); *The Santaland Diaries* (Birmingham Rep); *Rent* and *Cabaret* (English Theatre Frankfurt); *Bottle Universe* (Bush Theatre); *The Real Thing* (Theatre Royal, Bath UK tour); *Macbeth* and *La Sonnambula* (Opera Holland Park); *Anything Goes* (Mark Goucher UK tour); *Angels in America* (Crucible, Sheffield), *Horseplay* and *All Nighter* (Royal Ballet); *Love Me Tonight* (Hampstead); *The Lying Kind* (Royal Court); *Stitching* (Bush Theatre, Traverse Edinburgh, Berlin, Budapest)

Bob was awarded the Time Out Designer of The Year award for his Set Design for DV8's production of *The Happiest Day of My Life* in 1999.

TINA MACHUGH
LIGHTING DESIGNER

Tina's recent designs include *Alcina* and *Falstaff* (English Touring Opera); *When Harry met Sally* (No 1 tour); *Idomeneo* (Los Angeles Opera with Placido Domingo); *Arabian Nights*, *Merlin and the Winter King* and *A Midsummer Night's Dream* (Derby Playhouse); *The Hypochondriac* (Coventry Belgrade); *00:00:00:00: Timecode* (Royal Opera House Clore Studio); *Cold Comfort* and *A Number* (Prime Cut Theatre Company, Belfast); *Doldrum Bay* and *Done up like a Kipper* (Abbey, Dublin); *Vera of Las Vegas* (Opera Theatre Co Ireland); *Hans Christian Anderson* (Arc Dance) and *Book of Evidence* at the Kilkenny Arts Festival and Gate Theatre, Dublin (for which Tina was nominated for Best Lighting Design/Irish Times).

For the RSC she has lit *The Tempest*, *Love in a Wood*, *The Comedy of Errors*, *Henry VI* and *Ghosts* (Olivier Award nomination). She also had an Olivier Award nomination for her work on *Rutherford and Son* at the National Theatre.

COMPANY

SEAN PRITCHARD
SOUND DESIGNER

Sean is from Liverpool and studied
Production and Performance
Technology at The Liverpool Institute
for Performing Arts before taking
a job with the Everyman Theatre
in 1999. He is currently Chief
Technician at the Everyman.

Sound designs for the company
include: *Port Authority*, *Urban Legend*,
*The Kindness of Strangers; Fly; The
Mayor of Zalamea; A Little Pinch of
Chilli; 'Master Harold'... and the Boys,
The Tempest* and *Cinderella, the Rock
'n' Roll panto*.

BRIAN D HANLON
COSTUME SUPERVISOR

Brian graduated from Nottingham Trent
University with a BA Hons in Theatre
Design. His initial contact with the arts
occurred with his involvement with the
Everyman Youth Theatre.

As a Costume Supervisor he has
worked at the Royal National Theatre,
the Tricycle Theatre Kilburn and most
recently on *Falstaff* at the Guildhall
School of Music & Drama.

At the Liverpool Everyman and
Playhouse: *Billy Liar, Season's
Greetings, The Tempest, Chimps,
Who's Afraid of Virginia Woolf, Dr
Faustus, The Odd Couple, Ma
Rainey's Black Bottom, The
Astonished Heart/Still Life,
Breezeblock Park, Neville's Island,
Around the World in 80 Days,
Educating Rita, Popcorn, Les Liaisons
Dangereuses, Playboy of the Western
World* and *Puss in Blue Suede Boots*.

ADAM MAHER
ASSISTANT DIRECTOR

Adam trained in Directing at London's Central School of Speech and Drama, having previously studied bachelor degrees in Drama and Music at the Australian National University.

UK Theatre credits include:
Masterclass with Steven Pimlott and *Fresh Kills* (Theatre Royal Haymarket); Assistant Director to Pamela Howard *At The End of the Earth* (Ivy House); *Notes on Falling Leaves* (CSSD - London); devised piece: *Girl in Box* (CSSD - London).

Australian Theatre credits include:
Nightsongs (Street Theatre Studio); *Loot* (ANU Drama Lab); *Telling Moments* (Street Theatre Studio); *Boom-Bang-a-Bang* (Courtyard Theatre) and *Beautiful Thing* (Street Theatre Studio).

In 2004 Adam won the Australian Critics Circle award for his production of Jonathan Harvey's *Beautiful Thing*.

COMPANY THANKS

Mr. Silverberg of Silverberg Opticians

CREATE www.createuk.com a charity located in Speke that recycles white goods

Lacoste, Whitechapel, Liverpool.

STAFF

Paradise Bound

For our Angie

Characters

Ann Simpson (**Simmo**), *fifty, works in catering/silver service*
Kathleen Williams, *forty-seven, works in a cafe*
Danny Williams, *nineteen, works in construction*
Anthony Carter, *nineteen, works in telesales*

Special thanks to Suzanne Bell; I've never seen anyone work as hard as you, and I wouldn't be here without you, so thank you.

Thanks to Gemma and Deborah for making me feel like family.

Thanks to Victoria and Oonagh for endless cups of tea and words of encouragement.

Thanks to everyone at the Ev and Playhouse for constant support (especially Lizzie, Mike, Lou and Sarah and the marketing team).

Thank you Sue Dunderdale, Kerry Peers, Mary Jo Randle, Ciaran Griffiths and Michael Ryan – I'm very lucky.

Thank you so much Micheline Steinberg, Matt Connell and (the fabulous) Ginny Sennett

Special thanks to the inspirations – Mum, Dad, Nan, Grandad, all the girls, Barry, Shaun, Nicky, Carl, Michelle, Helen, Emma, Katie, Vicki, Wendy, Ian, Mark and Carol McLean and Pat Hart.

Scene One

The stage is divided between two sets. On the left is **Kathleen***'s kitchen, a long table to the front of the stage, a kitchen unit to the rear. On the right is a strip of turf sandwiched between two old buildings, a brand new bench parked in the middle of it. On either side of the turf stands wall-length wire fencing. It is afternoon. On the turf we find* **Danny** *and* **Anthony** *kicking a ball to each other. In the kitchen* **Kathleen** *is setting out plates and cutlery on the kitchen table. She is short and portly, with dark hair and olive skin. She wears a white overall from work.*

Ann *enters with a box filled with cartons of food. She is large and hefty, with blonde hair, and wears a loose-fitting blouse and skirt. She is swimming in jewellery.*

Ann   Eighteen quid! Not bad, really.

Kathleen   Didja get a menu?

Ann   I've got one in the 'ouse, I'll bring it round.

They start to unwrap boxes of food and dish out. On the turf, **Anthony** *sits down on the bench.*

Danny   Well played before, lad.

Anthony   Knackered.

Danny   Thought yer were gonna break Fletcher's legs, the way yer went for it.

Beat.

Anthony   How long's this been 'ere?

Danny   Which?

Anthony   This. (*He stamps his foot on the turf.*) This.

Danny   Ages.

Anthony   It 'asn't! I woulda seen it.

Danny   It's been 'ere about a month. Don't get used to it, though, kid.

Anthony   What d'yer mean?

Danny *jabs a thumb in the direction of the fencing.*

Danny   That's my 'andiwork.

Anthony   That was quick, wasn' it?

Danny (*shrugs*)   Dave's 'ad the job lined up for ages, probably before they even laid the turf.

Anthony   That sounds about right. Put turf down, stick a bench on top of it, but get it fenced up before anyone gets a chance to . . .

Danny   To what? I'm surprised it doesn't stink'v piss already! (*He points to the fence to the left.*) We did that Thursday. (*To the right.*) That Friday.

Anthony (*laughs*)   Don't strain yerselves.

Danny   We're gonna put it up bit by bit.

Anthony   What's the point'v that?

Danny   Don't ask me, mate. Council, innit? I stopped askin' questions a long time ago. Plus . . . I don't care.

They both chuckle.

Pause.

Anthony   It was the launderette wasn' it?

Danny   Up until a month ago, yeah.

Anthony   They knocked it down to put a patch a' grass between the chippy an' the bettin' shop?

Danny   Capital of Culture, innit?

He reaches down and snatches up a few blades.

Anthony   It's too green.

Danny   Looks better than the arl bagwash, dunnit?

Anthony   Yeah, an' it's gonna look bloody marvellous once it's got that barbed-wire touch to it. Mind you, it'll look less outta place then . . .

Danny   Yeah, like you give a toss!

Anthony   Maybe I do.

Danny *stops in his tracks.*

Beat.

Danny   Let's go an' get some scran.

Anthony   Good idea, I'm wastin' away 'ere.

Danny *laughs.*

Kathleen *and* **Ann** *sit down as the lads move offstage.*

Throughout the next conversation they start to pick at the various meals. Sweet and sour chicken is placed in the middle, with three boxes of fried rice, curry king prawn, four portions of sui mai, two portions of crispy spring rolls, two portions of sesame prawn toast, beef and green pepper and two bags of chips. The smell fills the kitchen immediately.

Kathleen   Oh them sui mais are gorgeous!

Ann   Oh, me stomach's goin' off its 'ead.

Kathleen   Prawns look big in that curry.

Ann   Them spring rolls the Vietnam ones?

Kathleen   Vietnamese? No, they were too sweet.

Ann   I was gonna say, yeah.

Kathleen   Chips are pretty well done.

Ann   Good, don't like that other place with the warm-up chips they give yer.

Kathleen   They give yer a lot with the sweet an' sour, don't they?

Ann   Probably loadsa batter with a tiny bit a' chicken in the middle!

The back door opens and **Anthony** *and* **Danny** *enter.*

Danny   Ooooh!

Kathleen   Hiya love.

Anthony   Oh nice!

Ann   Piss off, you two, eatin' all my dinner on me!

Anthony   Come off it, Simmo, even you couldn' eat all that.

Ann   'Ey, yer cheeky get!

Kathleen *laughs.* **Danny** *passes through with the ball.*

Kathleen   Get the ball out me kitchen, Dan.

Danny *(exits)*   What I'm doin'!

Kathleen   Anthony, get that soy sauce for us, lad.

Ann   Where've you two been?

Anthony   Astro.

Ann *(sarcastically)*   *How* old are yers?

Anthony   Nineteen.

Danny *(offstage)*   Which means too old for you!

Ann   Hey!

Kathleen *and* **Anthony** *laugh.* **Anthony** *takes the soy sauce out of one of the cupboards and passes it over to* **Kathleen**.

Kathleen   Wanna glass of wine?

Anthony   Na, 'ave yer got anythin' softer?

Kathleen   Coke in the fridge, 'elp yerself.

Anthony *goes to the fridge.*

Kathleen   There's cans a' Stella in there as well, y'know.

Danny *re-enters wearing a pair of track-suit bottoms instead of his shorts.*

Kathleen   I thought yer'd be back by now.

Danny   We got carried away.

Anthony *laughs.*

Danny   Anthony nearly broke Fletcher's leg.

Ann   Ah, now that's not nice!

Anthony (*laughing*)   I know . . .

Kathleen   How did that 'appen?!

Anthony   He got in the way.

Danny   Poor bastard didn't know what'd hit him.

He laughs.

Kathleen   Dirty, that! You weren't laughin' when it 'appened to you, were yer?

Danny *looks at her in surprise.*

Kathleen   That bloody agony you went through because someone'd got a bit overexcited with the ball. Weeks in 'ospital, Ann! Weeks!

Ann   Ah, I remember, terrible that!

Anthony   Ee are, Kath, I didn't do that much damage to Fletcher.

Kathleen   I'm sure yer didn't, lad.

Danny   But thanks for bringin' that up all the same, Mum.

Kathleen   What? I'm just sayin' . . .

Danny   All right, leave it.

Silence from all four for a moment. **Kathleen** *looks away.*

Ann (*nervous*)   Come on, then, don't stand eyein' it up, make yer move, boys!

Danny *and* **Anthony** *sit down opposite each other,* **Anthony** *passing him a drink.* **Danny** *snatches the drink off him.* **Ann** *and* **Kathleen** *sit at either end of the table.* **Danny** *tucks in immediately.*

Danny   Stingey with the sui mais, aren't they? Three in a portion?

Kathleen   They're friggin' massive, that's why!

Danny   Where d'yer order from?

Kathleen   Shanghai Garden.

Danny   Better from the Pekin'. You always order from the shit places!

Kathleen *looks at* **Ann** *and rolls her eyes.*

Ann   The Pekin' shut on Sundays now.

Danny   Yeah, even they 'ave their roast.

Anthony *laughs, as does* **Ann**.

Kathleen   I made a roast on Wednesday!

Danny   Who the fuck makes a roast on a Wednesday? It was left over from the café!

Kathleen   Lovely leg of lamb, Ann.

Ann   Mmm.

Kathleen   The smack'eads who come in the café were sellin' them.

Danny   Yer bought food off them dirty bitches?

Kathleen   It was all sealed, they'd only just robbed them out the Kwikky over the road.

Anthony   'Ope yer checked it for syringes.

Ann *laughs, biting into a spring roll.*

Danny   Where'd they 'ide a syringe in a leg a' lamb, yer tool?!

Kathleen   'Ey!

Anthony *laughs,* **Danny** *shakes his head with a chuckle.* **Ann** *looks at the spring roll she's eating.*

Ann   Don' 'alf know 'ow to cook, them Chinks.

Anthony's *fork screeches on his plate on the word 'Chinks' and the women suck air in through their teeth. He clears his throat.*

Anthony   So where'd yers go last night, ladies?

Ann   Ladies?

Kathleen   He means me.

Ann   Ah.

Laughter all around.

Kathleen   We ended up in Flares. Dive.

Ann   Good laugh, though, weren' it?

Kathleen   What, apart from the dirty Turk all over me most the night?

Danny   Don't be bringin' a Turk 'ome 'ere!

Kathleen   Oh, as if!

Anthony   Still got it, then, Kath?

Kathleen   Oh yes, lad, only it's with the wrong friggin' fellers!

Ann   Bit of an improvement in the Jacaranda, weren't they, kid?

Kathleen   The ones who weren't fifteen?

Ann   I'm sayin' nothin'.

Danny   An' don't think yer bringin' anyone in 'ere who's younger than me!

Ann   Don't worry, lad, I wouldn't let 'er. She can take 'im back to mine.

They all burst out laughing. Except for **Danny**.

Danny   Doesn't surprise me.

Ann   Hey!

Kathleen   As if I would, Danny, what d'yer take me for?

Danny *falls silent, continues to eat.* **Kathleen** *laughs.*

Kathleen   I think you're a cheeky bastard.

Danny   Why, 'cos I don't want you slappin' it about town?

Kathleen   There's a difference between slappin' it about an' . . .

Ann   Lettin' someone buy yer a drink!

Silence.

Danny   Who bought yer a drink?

Kathleen   Oh, call the police, some cunt bought me a brandy an' Coke!

Danny   Who?!

Kathleen   Ann, what was 'is name?

Ann   Karl.

Danny   Karl?

Kathleen   He was nice!

Danny   I don't wanna know!

Ann   Yer just asked!

Kathleen   I'm sure he was married.

Anthony   What made yer think that?

Kathleen   Little tan line on 'is finger.

Danny   Dirty bastard.

Kathleen   Still let 'im buy me a drink.

Danny   Fuck's sake.

Ann   It's not like she shagged 'im!

Danny (*disgusted*)   Ah!

Kathleen   Listen, lad, I can't 'elp it, yer mother's irresistible! Deal!

Danny   Not that irresistible, clearly.

Ann   'Ang on!

Kathleen   Leave it, Ann. That's for the football comment, isn' it?

Danny *is quiet.*

Kathleen   So I'll let yer off.

Ann   Weren't you boys out last night?

Anthony   Yeah.

Ann   Any good?

Anthony   It was OK, like.

Danny   Too many dirty old women about.

Kathleen *looks at* **Ann** *and they both roll their eyes.*

Kathleen   Where d'yers go?

Danny   All over the place.

Anthony   Usual crap. Concert Square, Slater Street . . .

Ann   Oh, surprised yer never saw us . . .

Danny   Or 'eard yers.

Kathleen   Don't yer like them places, Ant?

Anthony *shrugs.*

Danny   Anthony's a cut above them places now, aren't yer, lad?

Ann   Yer what, all them little girls runnin' round with their tits out everywhere?

Anthony *laughs, shifts in his seat slightly.*

Ann   Don't know 'ow their mothers let them walk out the 'ouse like that!

Danny   Like you wouldn't show it off if yer still could?

Ann   Hey you, who said I can't?

Anthony   Fuckin' environmental 'ealth . . .

Laughter all around.

Only kiddin', Simmo.

Ann   I know yer are, my tits are fabulous.

Beat.

So, have you two got girlfriends yet?

They both fall silent.

Ha! That shut yers up!

Anthony   I'm still in recovery, Simmo.

Danny   Yeah, he's still pussy-whipped from the last one.

Ann   That 'alf-caste girl wear yer out, lad?

Anthony   We just . . . wanted different things.

Danny   Yeah, you wanted someone who wasn't a bitch.

Ann   She 'ave a chip on 'er shoulder?

Anthony   Erm . . .

Ann   I mean, she was beautiful, but they're all like that. Don't know whether they're black or white so they take it out on the rest of us poor bastards.

Danny *laughs and concentrates on his eating.*

Anthony   She was just . . . mad, really.

Kathleen   Plenty more fish in the sea.

Ann   Plenty more dogs in the kennels.

Danny   Got that right.

Ann   Woulda thought you two'd cop off every time yer wen' out.

Danny   We do!

Anthony   Danny copped off last night, didn' yer, Dan?

Danny   Shut up.

Ann   Are you tryin' to come across as shy?

Kathleen   What was she like?

Danny   Can't remember.

Kathleen   Nice that, isn' it?

Ann   What d'yer expect? They're men!

Anthony   I thought she was nice. She's studyin' to be a doctor.

Danny *looks at him like he's an alien.*

Kathleen   Woman with brains, eh?

Ann   Must be a threat.

Danny   'Ow did yer know she was studyin' to be a doctor?

Anthony   Erm . . . little thing called a conversation.

Ann   He's a gentleman, aren't yer, Ant?

Danny   He's a tool.

Anthony (*laughs*)   Cheeky bastard.

Kathleen   Daniel, there's nothin' wrong with a man who wants to talk to a woman before he gets into 'er knickers!

Ann   As long as he *gets* into 'er knickers after the conversation.

More laughter.

Anthony   Time for a toilet break, I think.

He dashes out of the room as **Ann** *and* **Kathleen** *laugh.*

Ann   He's lovely, isn' he?

Danny   Borin' bastard last night, though.

Kathleen   Ah, he's probably a bit lost without Lisa.

Danny   They were only together a year!

Ann   Hey, a year's a long time!

Kathleen   Especially for you, yer two-week wonder.

Ann   Someone's ate the last of the sweet an' sour.

Danny   Relationships are just too much stress.

Kathleen   Tell me about it.

Danny   I never meet anyone worth stickin' it out for.

Kathleen   Yer will.

Ann   Then the cunt'll leave yer for a younger model.

Kathleen *laughs and* **Danny** *rolls his eyes.*

Ann   Na, you find the right girl, take yer time. Ignore us.

Danny   I always do, Simmo.

Ann   Cheek.

Kathleen   I don't know if I can be bothered goin' out tonight if I'm 'onest.

Danny   You two aren't goin' back out!

Ann   What's wrong with that, like?

Danny   Why are you goin' out again?

Ann   People to see!

Danny   Like who? Like Karl?

Kathleen   Grow up, Danny!

Danny   You're a fine one to talk about growin' up!

Ann   Excuse me! You an' Anthony are back out tonight, aren't yers?

Danny   What's that got to do with it?

Ann   What's good enough for the goose!

Danny   Goose is right.

Kathleen   Less of the goosin', please, I'm tryin' to eat me dinner.

Danny   Shut up.

Kathleen   Have yer 'eard the way he speaks to me, Ann? That's what I'm rearin'!

Danny *laughs, as does* **Ann**. **Kathleen** *shakes her head, eats in silence.* **Anthony** *enters with a smile.*

Anthony   What've a' missed?

Danny   Sweet an' sour, kid.

Scene Two

Lights up on the turf. It's evening. **Anthony** *enters, dressed from a night out. He looks a little wasted. He sits down on the bench, laughing to himself. He leans forward, elbows on knees, sighs. He sits back and looks up at the sky. After a moment he raises his hand, shaped like a gun with his forefinger, and shoots at the stars.*

Danny (*offstage*)   Whatta you playin' at, yer knob?

He enters from the right, also dressed from a night out. Also drunk, although not as far gone as **Anthony**.

Anthony   All right, lad?

Danny   Am *I* all right?

Anthony (*laughs*)   What?

Danny   Who was on the phone?

Anthony *hesitates.*

Danny   Is someone dead?

Anthony   No, it's nothin' like that . . .

Danny (*laughing*)   Coulda fooled me, yer drama queen.

Anthony *looks up at him with a drunken grin.*

Danny *sits down next to him.*

Danny   Was it Lisa?

Anthony *looks at him and shakes his head.*

Anthony   Wow, are you obsessed with 'er or what?

Danny   Y'what?

Anthony   Every little thing, it's, 'Is it Lisa?'

Danny   Ee are, yer prick, yer just broke up with the girl, I'm tryin' to be sensitive.

Anthony *bursts out laughing, and* **Danny** *starts to get wound up, embarrassed.*

Danny   Fuck off!

He stands.

Anthony (*mimics*)   *I'm tryin' to be sensitive!*

Danny   So tell me what's goin' on with yer, then!

Silence from **Anthony**. **Danny** *throws a foot up on the bench.*

Danny   I know somethin's up.

Anthony (*laughs*)   Why does somethin' 'ave to be up just 'cos I'm bored of doin' the same shit all the time?

Danny   Well, somethin' must be up for yer to be 'avin' little secret phone calls an' runnin' off like a woman.

Anthony *laughs, looking off into the distance.*

Danny   Whatever, kid . . .

He steps back.

Anthony   I'm gettin' off.

Danny   What, yer in a huff now?

Anthony   No, I mean I'm gonna get off, proper!

He gets up off the bench and walks to the edge of the turf.

Danny   Whatta yer talkin' about?

Anthony   Remember me tellin' yer about Australia?

Danny *is quiet. He approaches* **Anthony**, *who keeps his back to him.*

Anthony   They granted me a visa. Soft bastards.

Danny   Yer mean . . . to go out there?

Anthony *nods.*

Danny   Go to Australia? An' then what?

Anthony   I told yer about Helen in work, didn' I? I told yer ages ago . . .

Danny   The lesbian?

Anthony   Not that that's even relevant, but . . .

Danny (*mimics*)   *Not that that's . . .*

Anthony   Do you wanna know or what?! About what she was sayin', about 'er mate who lives in Queensland . . .

Danny   I can't remember, kid . . .

Anthony   No, why would yer? It was just . . . talk.

Danny   What, an' now it's not, then?

Anthony *shrugs again, then turns to look at* **Danny**.

Danny   Who's 'er mate?

Anthony   Some feller, he's got pubs all over the place . . . different parts a' Queensland an' that.

Danny   Oh, right.

Anthony   He's gonna need staff for, like, over Christmas an' that . . . an' then after a few months there'll be jobs openin' up in his other places, he's openin' new bars in the New Year, like . . .

Danny   An' yer've got this visa to go an' work for 'im? So what was the phone call?

Anthony   Helen. I phoned her yesterday to say me approval letter 'ad come, an' she's 'ad a word with this feller. He said he can only keep the job open for me till the end of October.

Danny *looks at him.*

Anthony   Yeah.

Danny   Shit, kid!

Anthony *laughs nervously.*

Danny   Talk about last-minute!

Anthony   Decision time, innit?

Danny   Well, yer've got yer visa an' everythin' . . . All yer've gotta do now is . . .

Anthony   Go.

Danny *falls silent.* **Anthony** *grins, a look of indecision on his face.*

Danny   Australia.

Anthony *nods, smiling.*

Danny   The sun.

Anthony   Surf.

Danny   Birds.

Anthony *nods, closing his eyes.* **Danny** *looks at him quizzically.*

Anthony   No more of this sad, fuckin' joke . . .

Danny   Eh?

Anthony   This.

He kicks the turf. **Danny** *shrugs.*

Danny   Jib this, I'm destroyed, mate.

He stands.

Anthony   Must be gettin' old.

He offers his hand to **Anthony**, *who takes hold of it with a smile and a sigh.* **Danny** *drags him to his feet and pats him on the back.*

Danny   Full'v surprises, you, innit?

Anthony   I am, yeah.

He laughs, looking down at his feet.

Danny   Strewth, mate!

Anthony *laughs again, as does* **Danny**.

Danny   You stayin' in ours?

Anthony   Er . . .

Danny   We just walked past yours so I take it yer are.

Anthony *laughs and shrugs.*

Danny   Thought so. Prick.

Anthony   Dick'ead.

They laugh at each other as they exit the turf. Lights down on the turf as the kitchen is illuminated.

Scene Three

In the kitchen, **Kathleen** *enters, slightly staggering. She is dressed up but slightly dishevelled.* **Ann** *follows suit, dressed similarly, a cigarette hanging out of her mouth, rooting in her handbag.*

Kathleen   Me feet are killin' me.

She heads for the fridge.

Ann (*sitting down*)   Meet yer mate. Get the cans out, Kath.

Kathleen   Don't know if I feel sick.

Ann   You always feel bloody sick, yer lightweight.

Kathleen   Starvin' as well.

Ann   That's why yer feel sick, yer've bin drinkin' all night an' yer 'aven' ate.

Kathleen   What, yer mean apart from the dirty great Chinese banquet we 'ad this avvy?

Ann   Oh aye, yeah.

Kathleen *passes her a can of Stella and gets two glasses out of the dishwasher.*

Ann   Either that or butterflies . . .

Kathleen   Be'ave!

Ann (*laughs*)   Oh look at yer, blushin'!

Kathleen   I am not blushin'!

Ann   Yes you are! You like 'im, don't yer?

Kathleen   Of course I bloody like 'im, if I didn't I wouldn' 'ave met him again, would I?

Ann   All right, don't get yer knickers in a twist!

Kathleen *throws a funny look.*

Ann   That's if they're still on!

Kathleen   Hey, yer know yer own tricks best, Simmo!

Ann   I friggin' wish.

They fall silent for a moment.

Kathleen   Didn't yer like that Pedro feller?

Ann   Na, I was only killin' time while you were coppin' off with lover boy.

Kathleen   Stop it, yer make us sound like teenagers, Ann!

Ann   Nothin' wrong with that, girl.

They both laugh.

Tell yer what, he's nice, though.

Kathleen *takes a swig of her drink.*

Ann   Not that I've 'ad the best judgement with men in the past, like. But I'd never see you get 'urt by one of them.

Kathleen   Not again, anyway.

Ann   Yeah.

Silence.

It's all right that yer scared, y'know, girl.

Kathleen   Who said I'm scared?

Ann   Who said I was born yesterday, Kath?

Kathleen *chuckles.*

Kathleen   Packed tonight, wasn' it?

Ann *rolls her eyes.*

Kathleen   OK, he's nice an' I like 'im an' I might be a bit nervous! Now can we change the fuckin' subject?

Ann   OK, OK. Yeah, it was packed.

Kathleen   What was that Tea Factory like, Ann!

Ann   How the fuck did we end up in there, Kath?

Kathleen   You an' your ideas, 'Let's get Cosmo's, girl!'

Ann   I just fancied a bit of a change.

Kathleen   Who d'yer think yer are? Jessica friggin' Parker?

Ann *(laughs)*   Five quid for a glass of nail-varnish remover.

Kathleen   Oh it took the linin' off me throat, that shite! Lovely frosted glass as well . . .

Ann   I know, it looked gorgeous!

Kathleen   That's what it's all about now, innit? The way it looks. The image!

Ann   Capital of Culture, girl, polish everythin', make it look shinier than it really is.

Kathleen   God, they'll be shippin' the Brasso in crate by crate.

Ann   Needs more than Brasso.

Kathleen   Hey, it needs more than Urban Flash flats in Duke Street an' poncey bars down the Dock for up their own ass, coke-snortin' dick'eads . . .

Ann   An' a Harvey Nicks on Paradise Street!

Kathleen   What bastard can afford to shop there?

Ann   Hilarious, isn' it?

Kathleen   An' do they do anythin' for us round 'ere?

Ann   They put a bench on Mill Street.

Kathleen   What the fuck's a bench gonna do on Mill Street?

Ann   Somewhere to sit.

Kathleen   Somewhere to sit?

Ann   Yeah, well, when yer can't get a cab after a night out an' yer 'ave to walk all the way 'ome . . . don't yer just wish yer 'ad somewhere to sit?

Good night, though, wasn' it?

Kathleen   Once we got outta that Tea Factory. Couldn't be doin' with places like that. Yer go out to 'ave a laugh, not . . .

Ann   Stand there like one a' Lewis's.

Kathleen   They were scared to bloody smile, 'alf a' them!

Ann   Probably too drugged up to smile, girl.

Kathleen   Shame, isn' it, Ann?

Ann   'At's the way they are now. They don't go out an' get pissed like we do, they go out an' take their tablets an' their speed an' shove shit up their nostrils.

Kathleen   Stick bottles in each other's faces.

Ann   Them girls on Bold Street were absolutely vile, weren't they?

Kathleen   Oh Ann, that turned my stomach!

Ann   Fightin' with bottles an' glasses, what 'appened to good old-fashioned slappin' an' punchin'?

The microwave pings and they both jump.

They're no better than the bloody fellers. My belly thinks me throat's bin cut 'ere.

Kathleen   I know. Ow!

She gets a tea towel to pick up the hot plate. **Ann** *gets up and gets out some cutlery, as well as two more cans of Stella. They carry the plates to the table and sit.*

Ann   Thank God for the Jacaranda. And you know who.

Kathleen   Hmm . . .

Ann   Oh Kath, he's nice! Don't yer wanna be 'appy?

Kathleen   I wanna be 'appy, Ann, it's just . . . the 'assle.

Ann   'Assle? 'Assle's what it's all about!

Kathleen   I've 'ad it up to 'ere with it, girl.

Ann   I'm not talkin' about that kind of 'assle, I'm talkin' about . . .

Kathleen (*nods*)   Proper . . . hassle.

Ann   Let's face it, you wouldn' 'ave took 'is number if you didn't want to . . . y'know.

She reaches across the table and picks up **Kathleen**'s *mobile.*

Kathleen   Whatta yer . . . 'ey!

She grabs for the phone and **Ann** *sits back in her seat, giggling, holding the phone up.*

Kathleen   Ann, give us it!

Ann   Where's my glasses?

She reaches into her bag and takes her glasses out.

Kathleen   Ee are, give us it back, Ann, come on.

Ann   I'm not gonna do anythin'! Where is it then . . . contacts, right . . .

Kathleen   I swear to God, if you ring 'im . . .

Ann   What do you take me for, Kathleen Williams? There it is . . . ahh . . . Karl with a K.

Kathleen   Pass it.

Ann   How d'yer . . .

Kathleen   Simmo.

Ann   Chill out, will yer?

Kathleen   Whatta yer tryin' to do?

Ann   I'm terrible at textin' people!

Kathleen *stands immediately and rushes to grab the phone from her.* **Ann** *howls with laughter as* **Kathleen** *takes the phone.*

Ann   Oh, I'm windin' yer up!

Kathleen   You've got my nerves gone, you!

Ann   You should send 'im a little message, though.

Kathleen   Do one.

Ann   Bit a' text-sex!

They both burst out laughing. The back door opens. Enter **Danny** *and* **Anthony**.

Danny   Aye aye, what's all the noise about?

Anthony   Don't stop on account of us, ladies.

Kathleen   Oh ee are!

Ann   Smell the food, did yers, yer drunken bastards?

Anthony *and* **Danny** *descend on the leftovers.*

Anthony   Nice one.

Danny   The Bo Tan was shut.

Ann   Not like them Turks to be shut any day of the week.

Danny   The window was all cracked, there must've bin a fight in there or somethin'.

Kathleen   Oh, isn' it vile, Ann!

Anthony *bites into a spring roll and moans with satisfaction.*

Ann *pulls a letter out of her bag.*

Ann   Oh, I meant to show yer this, Kath.

Kathleen   What is it?

Ann   It's from our Ronnie's kids . . .

Kathleen   Oh, in Australia?

Danny (*quietly*)   Not another one.

Anthony *laughs. He looks at* **Danny**, *who isn't as amused.*

Ann   They even wrote the address out on the envelope! Not that that they shoulda bothered, they coulda wrote 'Ann Simpson – The Usual' an' it woulda got to me!

They laugh.

Danny   I'm goin' to bed.

He heads for the door, plate in hand.

You comin' up, Ant?

Ann *wolf whistles.* **Anthony** *chuckles, pouring himself a drink.*

Danny   Piss off.

Ann   So sweet!

Kathleen   Aye aye!

Anthony   Be up in a minute.

Danny   What, after they've bored you to death about the land down under?

Anthony *laughs.*

Kathleen   Not everyone thinks we're borin' old fishwives yer know, lad.

Ann   Not even yer boyfriend!

Anthony *almost spits his drink out.*

Danny   Whatever.

Anthony *looks at him with a bashful grin.* **Danny** *shakes his head. He leaves, embarrassed, as the ladies laugh.*

Anthony   How old are they now?

Ann   Seven an' eight.

She hands the letter to **Kathleen**.

Ann   Look at the picture they drew.

Kathleen   Ah, the beach.

Ann   They're askin' me to go an' see them in the summer.

Kathleen   Well, bloody get over there! An' take me with yer!

She sighs with a smile and passes the letter back.

God, can yer blame them?

Anthony   When yer live in a dump like this?

Kathleen   Excuse me, sunshine, I hope you're not talkin' about my palace!

Anthony *laughs.*

Anthony   Don't be daft, Kath.

He leans against the sink and looks out the window.

I mean out there.

He stares off for a moment as **Kathleen** *and* **Ann** *are silent.*

Ann   Imagine the heat over there.

Kathleen *sighs.*

Ann   All them new faces.

Anthony *smiles to himself.*

Ann   All that space.

Kathleen *hums her agreement.*

Ann   I'd be lost.

Anthony *looks around at them.*

Ann   I wouldn't know what to do with meself!

Anthony   I reckon yer would.

Ann   Do yer, lad?

He nods.

Anthony   I'm goin' up.

Ann   Ah, goodnight, God bless.

Anthony   'Night.

Kathleen   'Night, lad.

He exits. **Ann** *lights a cigarette.*

Kathleen   He'll get in with our Danny as usual so you can 'ave Chris's bed.

Ann   Good of them, givin' an arl woman a bed.

Kathleen   There's a VO there from Chris. Third one he's sent out for our Danny, y'know . . .

Ann   He still not gone up to see 'im?

Kathleen   An' I can't be doin' with it this week, the way my 'ead is.

Silence.

Isn't that terrible, girl?

Ann   Is it shite, you've done enough for that lad, Kathleen.

Kathleen   It never seems to be enough, though, does it?

Ann   Listen, the most important thing . . . live yer life.

Kathleen *nods, taking a pull of her cigarette.*

Ann   It's too bloody short!

She taps her finger on **Kathleen***'s mobile phone.* **Kathleen** *looks up with a nervous grin and exhales a cloud of smoke.*

Lights down.

Scene Four

Lights up on the kitchen. It's the next morning and **Kathleen** *is in her dressing-gown, rushing around, trying to iron her overall for work at the same time as making a cup of tea. She takes toast from the toaster, puts it on a plate and butters it. She looks at her watch and groans. She picks up the cordless telephone from the kitchen table and dials.*

Danny *enters, with his shirt from last night hanging loose. He grabs the toast.*

Kathleen (*into phone*)   Yeah, I'm gonna be in at ten. I told yer. No, I told yer.

Danny   Tell the bastard to . . .

Kathleen   Yeah. Doctor's appointment. At nine, why?

Danny *looks at her in surprise.*

Kathleen   Just an appointment. I stayed late on Friday, remember? Yeah. OK.

She hangs up with force.

Cheeky Turkish bastard! 'Why you have appointment, Kathleen?'

Danny   You're a fool for lettin' them treat you like that!

Kathleen   Oh I'm a fool am I? I'll fuck it off then, shall I? Seein' as we're friggin' made of money!

Danny   All right, chill out, woman.

Kathleen   Don't 'woman' me!

Beat.

Danny   There's some problem with the contractors that's gonna take all day to sort so there's no point me goin' in.

Kathleen   At least one of us gets a day off. Put some more bread in that toaster for me, seein' as yer've just 'elped yerself to mine!

He sighs and gets some bread as she starts ironing. He stands in her way as he moves towards the toaster.

Budge!

Danny   Ee are, steady on.

Kathleen   I'll steady you in a minute!

Danny *looks confused. He moves out of her way.*

Kathleen   Ah, my 'ead's wrecked.

Danny   Maybe if yer weren' out till all hours with the other one yer wouldn't be rushin' so much!

Kathleen   Don't start me while I've got the iron in me 'and, lad!

Danny *laughs.*

Kathleen   I'll go out an' get pissed if I want to! Believe me, I'm sick of sittin' around waitin' for other people! I'll do whatta like!

She holds up her overall to look over it. She tuts, turns it over and lays it over the ironing board. She looks at the toaster. She nudges past him and takes the toast out to butter it herself.

Danny   Suppose she's in our Chris's bed again?

Kathleen   Yeah.

Danny   As usual.

Kathleen   Bit like Anthony, then?

He falls silent.

Get us two paracetamol out, make yerself useful!

She bites into her toast, then carries on with her ironing.

You gonna go an' see our Chris when the lads go up?

Danny   Doubt it. So who was buyin' yer drinks this time?

Kathleen   Why d'yer doubt it? Yer 'aven't seen 'im since last month!

Danny   I'm sure he'll survive. Wrecks me 'ead, anyway.

Kathleen   That's your brother you're talkin' about!

Danny   Stop changin' the subject!

Kathleen   I'm not changin' the subject, I'm talkin' about our Chris!

Danny   An' I'm talkin' about you!

Kathleen   What?

Danny   Did yer see that feller again?

Silence. Ironing.

That a yes, then?

More silence as the ironing becomes more fervent.

Don't think yer bringin' 'im back 'ere.

She sighs as she continues to iron.

Yer wanna tell 'er where to go!

Kathleen   You wanna watch what you're sayin', lad.

She finishes her ironing.

Danny   D'yer blame me? The way she carries on?

Kathleen   Hang on! So it's all right for you an' your mates to go out an' get rotten an' cop off with all kinds but it's not for Ann or meself?

Danny   Yer middle-aged women!

Kathleen   An' what? I'm a middle-aged woman who's spent all 'er life lookin' after other people, an' what've I got to show for it?

Silence.

Danny   Yer used to know the difference.

Kathleen   What bloody difference?

Danny Between a woman who goes out an' 'as a laugh an' a woman who goes out an' makes a show of 'erself.

Kathleen Shhh! She's right upstairs!

Danny I'm not just talkin' about Ann.

Kathleen *sighs.*

Danny I don't want me mates thinkin' you're the same as 'er.

Kathleen She's been bloody good to me since yer dad went!

Danny Don't I know it!

Kathleen Meanin'?

Danny Meanin' he moved out an' she fuckin' moved in!

Kathleen She keeps me company just like Anthony keeps you company!

Danny Anthony doesn't give me a reputation!

Kathleen That girl doesn't give me one! She's livin' 'er life an' it's no other janglin' bastard's business what she does! Just like it's none of their business what *I* do!

Danny It's mine, though.

He looks round at **Kathleen**. *She stops, looks back at him. They both fall silent. An awkward moment is totally obliterated when* **Anthony** *dashes through from one door to the other, dragging his shirt on.*

Anthony Fuck fuck fuck!

They are both startled. He exits without another word.

Danny Forgot to set the alarm.

Kathleen *sighs, and goes to grab her overall.*

Danny Oh, will yer run the iron over me T-shirt for us?

Kathleen Do yer own shirt!

She takes her overall and exits. **Danny** *clears his throat and picks his T-shirt up from the back of a chair.*

Scene Five

The scene cuts between the turf and the kitchen.

It is late afternoon on the turf. Further fencing has been erected to the left of the turf, and is beginning to infringe on the kitchen. The sun is in the sky but is becoming increasingly low. We hear laughter offstage until **Danny** *and* **Anthony** *enter.* **Danny** *is in track-suit bottoms and a T-shirt and* **Anthony** *is in shorts and T-shirt. Both have just finished a game of football and are breathless.* **Danny** *holds the ball;* **Anthony** *is carrying a litre bottle of water.*

Danny   I was all over him like a fly on shit!

Anthony   No, it was well played, kid, I've gotta hand it to yer.

Danny   Was there ever any doubt?

Anthony   Well, it was lookin' ropey there for a minute, like.

Danny *gives an outraged laugh.* **Anthony** *laughs and sits down on the bench, taking a swig of water.*

Anthony   Hey, weren't we sittin' 'ere pissed last night?

Danny   Well, *you* were pissed.

Anthony   Yeah, I remember. Well, sort of.

Danny   Not much to remember, kid, yer didn't make any fuckin' sense.

Anthony *laughs.* **Danny** *sits down next to him, takes the bottle, swigs from it.*

Anthony   Since when 'ave I made sense?

Danny   Good point.

Anthony *watches him as he drinks.*

Anthony   Whatta yer up to tonight?

Danny *shrugs.*

Anthony   Wanna go the pictures?

Danny   What's on?

Anthony *Jarhead?*

Danny Ah yeah, I wanted to see that. About the squaddies?

Anthony Yeah, Jake Gyllenhaal's in it.

Danny looks at him with a frown.

Anthony *Donnie Darko.*

Danny Right, yeah.

Anthony It's on in FACT.

Danny FACT?

Anthony Where we went to see that exhibition?

Danny Where you *dragged* me to see that exhibition, yer mean?

Anthony Yer liked it!

Danny I was stoned!

Anthony *laughs.*

Danny It isn't subtitled like that other piece of crap last week, is it?

Anthony What's wrong with subtitles, like?

Danny Nothin', I just 'ave to be in the mood to fuckin' read as well as watch a film.

Anthony It's not subtitles.

Danny Bet you wish it was, though, Mr Culture.

They are silent for a moment.

Lights up on the kitchen. Nobody is on stage. After a moment the back door opens and **Kathleen** *and* **Ann** *enter carrying two bin-bags each.*

Ann He wants to be a bit more careful, just draggin' these out in the middle of the estate!

Kathleen Skiddy's bin doin' it for bloody years, Ann, he's an old pro!

Ann   God, it's like we've just been the bagwash.

They drag the bags over to the kitchen table and sit down.

If they hadn't knocked it down.

Kathleen   He said it's all out of the Wade's sale. He doesn't usually sell shite, like.

Ann   Yeah, he just talks it . . .

The turf.

Danny   We could just go out an' get pissed, I suppose.

Anthony   What, yer mean for a change?

Danny *laughs.*

Anthony   Na, I think I'm gonna try an' go into work without a hangover in the mornin'.

Danny   Ah, poor little you, 'avin' to go an' sit on yer arse all day with a hangover. Try puttin' a fuckin' fence up with one like I do.

Pause.

Ann *takes out a shirt and starts to take the plastic wrapping off it.*

Ann   What are they again?

Kathleen   The shirts are Burberry, I think he said.

Ann *takes her glasses out of her bag and puts them on before holding the shirt up to look at the label.*

Ann   Oh aye, yeah.

She examines the label.

The turf.

Danny   When are you 'andin' yer notice in?

Anthony *looks away.*

Danny   Or was that just talk?

Anthony   Was it, shite!

Danny   I thought it was all a big rush!

Anthony   It is.

Danny   So've yer told that girl when yer goin'?

Anthony   Not yet, no.

Danny   Why not?

Anthony   I've got shit to sort out!

Danny   Like what?

Anthony   Just shit!

Danny *is quiet.*

The kitchen.

Kathleen   They *are* lovely, like. There's Versace ones as well, but I think they're a bit girly.

Ann   Oh they're all girly now, it's the style.

Kathleen   I know.

The turf. **Anthony** *clears his throat.*

Anthony   Gotta tell me mum an' dad.

Danny   They'll be made up.

Anthony (*laughs*)   Yeah. Over the moon.

Danny *watches him curiously. He laughs.*

Danny   See that twat on the astro before?

Anthony   Who?

Danny   Y'know, Last of the Mohicans.

Anthony   I thought it looked cool.

Danny   Yeah, havin' a bit of a Mohican's one thing, but pink?

Anthony *shrugs.*

Danny   He loved 'imself to death!

He looks to **Anthony** *for a response. He takes a swig from the bottle of water.*

Anthony   It was red.

Danny   Come again?

Anthony   It wasn't pink, it was red.

Danny   Oh right. Didn't look that close.

Anthony   Good player, though.

Danny   Again, didn't look that close.

Anthony *looks at him for a second, then takes the bottle and swigs.*

Danny   Twat, though. Who bounces down Park Road with a pin . . . red Mohican?

Anthony *laughs, shakes his head.*

Danny   What?

Anthony *is silent for a moment.*

Danny   Is that your next move then, Mr Re-invention? Little Mohican number, hot pink?

Anthony   Fuck off.

Danny *laughs to himself.*

Anthony   Dick.

Danny   Suck it.

Anthony *is silent, looks away. He laughs, then looks back at* **Danny**.

Anthony   Hey, what if I did?

Danny   Did what?

Anthony   Bounced down Park Road with a pink Mohican? Can yer imagine what the lads'd say?

Danny   You'd look like a ponce!

Anthony   Who's to say I don't wanna look like that? Who's to say I don't wanna look different?

Danny Do yer?

Anthony I never said that, I just mean . . .

Silence, **Danny** *watching* **Anthony**.

The kitchen.

Ann Nice, that one.

Kathleen Which?

Ann The beige.

Kathleen Yeah, our Danny 'asn' seen them yet.

Ann He'll like loadsa these, he's dead trendy, isn' he?

Kathleen Gets that from me.

Ann *laughs. She continues to drag shirts out of the bag.*

Kathleen Is that a laugh?

Ann Y'what?

Kathleen Your face's bin trippin' yer this avvy!

Ann Just tired.

Kathleen *nods.* **Ann** *looks a little self-conscious.*

Ann They are good lads, aren't they? Even if Skiddy is a gobshite.

Kathleen D'yer know what? I don't know what I'd do without them sometimes. They say yer find out who yer real friends are.

Ann Yeah, an' it usually ends up yer can count them on one 'and.

The turf.

Anthony Did yer say yer mum's getting clothes off Skiddy today?

Danny Yeah, but you know what Skiddy's like, it'll be all that girly shite.

Anthony *nods.*

Danny   You should like it!

Anthony *bursts out laughing.*

Anthony   Hey, you're one to talk!

Danny *looks down at his clothing.*

Danny   What?

Anthony   Yer such a fashion queen!

Danny   Fashion queen?!

Anthony   It might be trackies by day but it's a different story when we go out, innit? Mr Versace.

Danny   Gotta make an effort. An' what if I'm a fashion queen, what's that make you?

The kitchen. **Ann** *opens one of the other bags.*

Kathleen   They're the Versace ones.

Ann   *They* meant to be for fellers? Yer'd 'ave to be a poof to walk round wearin' that!

Kathleen   Well, I'm gonna take some up to Steven on Thursday.

Ann   Whatta yer gettin' done?

Kathleen   Just some layers, I think. Caramel.

Ann   Oh yeah, I like that on your 'air.

Kathleen   It's annoyin' me with this colour.

Ann   Can't go wrong with caramel, girl. Suits yer eyes.

Kathleen   I know. Ee are, 'elp me sort these into sizes.

They both start to sort through the tops.

The turf. **Anthony** *is silent. He smiles, shrugs, takes a swig of drink.*

Danny   Wasn't long ago you were Mr Lacoste, remember? Just because yer've ditched the trackies altogether doesn't make you any different to me.

Anthony   I never said it did!

Danny   What's with that, anyway?

Anthony   Which?

Danny   The change in image.

Anthony   I didn't know there was one. (*He leans forward.*) Didn't look that close!

Danny *sniggers, slaps his forehead.* **Anthony** *falls back with a laugh.*

Anthony   Lisa thought I was too old for trackies.

Danny   An' did Lisa get yer into watchin' films in FACT an' . . . drinkin' green tea in the Tea Factory?

Anthony *laughs.*

Anthony   Yer'll never let me live that one down, will yer?

Danny   Only 'cos the One Four's right round the corner an' yer made me miss the first ten minutes of the game because the shit hadn't brewed properly!

Anthony   Yer meant to let it settle!

Danny   Yer meant to down six pints while yer shoutin' at a projector screen! Yer tit!

Anthony *laughs louder, holding his stomach.*

Danny   Looked like a piss sample, anyway.

He stands, bouncing the ball on the floor. He throws the ball to **Anthony***, who laughs and catches it.*

Danny   Reckon they've got green tea in Australia?

Anthony *chuckles, dropping the ball to his feet.*

Anthony   I'll send yer a postcard an' let yer know.

He kicks the ball to **Danny***.*

Danny   If yer ever get there.

Anthony   Too fuckin' right I'll get there!

Danny *boots it back.* **Anthony** *kicks the ball back to* **Danny**.

Danny   Why d'you wanna go so badly?

Anthony   Look around yer, mate, an' ask me that again!

Danny *shrugs.*

Anthony   It's a fuckin' show, it's depressin'!

Danny   I suppose yer get used to it.

Anthony   That's what I don't want. I need more than . . .

Danny   What?

Anthony   I want more than . . . sittin' off gettin' stoned.
I want more than . . . goin' to the same office day in day out
to sell broadband to dick'eads who 'aven't got a clue what yer
goin' on about.

He falls silent and looks away. Silence lingers. He looks back up.

I wanna walk down the road an' not know where I'm gonna
end up.

Danny *remains silent.*

Anthony   I want real grass that goes on for miles. Not false
turf stuck in between a chippy an' a bettin' shop.

Danny *reaches into his sock and takes out a spliff.*

Danny   You slaggin' off our Capital of Culture developments?

Anthony   Na. Let them flatten the place. Tarmac over the
eyesores on Park Road an' Milly . . .

Danny   They'll leave the Florry up, though. As long as they
don't 'ave to do it up.

Anthony (*laughs*)   An' the Mecca.

They both laugh.

Danny   But they'll put some wanky bar next door.

Anthony   An' people'll be shoutin' *'Line!'* in both.

Danny *laughs.*

Anthony   Oh, how grim.

Danny   Park Road gets Urban Splashed!

Anthony *laughs.*

Anthony   The Banana Bunch gets bumped for a new branch of Starbucks.

Danny *laughs.*

Anthony   The fifty-pence shop becomes a Virgin Megastore.

More laughter.

An' Tracey's Cakes is suddenly a deli!

They chuckle and fall silent.

Danny *sparks up and takes a pull.* **Anthony** *joins him on the bench, holding the ball beneath his foot.*

The kitchen. **Ann** *picks up one of the tops.*

Ann   I wonder if our Jackie'd 'ave that one for her lad.

Kathleen   She might do.

Ann   Then again, as if I'd *see* our Jackie if it wasn't friggin' . . . Christmas or a funeral.

Kathleen   I think you get paranoid about them girls, Ann.

Ann   Oh, do yer now? Well next time it's someone's birthday an' I'm the one who doesn't get invited, tell me then that I'm bein' paranoid!

There is silence for a moment

Sorry, I'm just a bit chocker.

Kathleen   I'll keep a few of these separate, see what our Danny thinks.

Ann   What about his mates?

Kathleen   Yeah, well, they wear all that kinda stuff as well.

Ann   Oh well, there y'go.

Kathleen   I texted him.

Ann   What?

Kathleen *sits down.*

Ann   The other feller?

Kathleen *nods.*

Ann   And?

Kathleen   We're goin' out Friday night.

Ann   Oh fantastic! See, I told yer, didn't I? What did yer say to 'im?

Kathleen   I just said I 'ad a nice time an' wouldn't mind doin' it again! Tell yer what, it took me from the beginnin' of *Emmerdale* to the advert break on *Corrie* to write the fuckin' thing.

Laughter.

Ann   The drought's nearly over.

Kathleen   Oh 'ey Ann, it's been that long I need a friggin' tsunami! I'm spittin' feathers!

They fall about laughing.

Talk about wakin' the dead.

The turf.

Danny   I don't know what you're going on for. I mean, once yer out'v 'ere yer won' 'ave to worry about – (*He chuckles.*) – the rapid decline of our fair ghetto.

Anthony   Wish it was that easy.

Danny   What's stoppin' yer?

Anthony   I don't know.

Danny   What's yer rush then? Stick around. Have a few kids!

Anthony   Fuck that!

Danny   Kids?

Anthony   Not just kids! What comes with them?

Danny hands him the spliff. He takes a pull.

Anthony   Bein' attached to some bird who's attached to a pram that's attached to a baby that's attached to a cheese an' onion pasty . . .

Danny   A Sayers kid!

Anthony   Trampin' 'round the Kwikky with all the other mothers . . .

Danny   Weekly school reunion.

Anthony   Swear to God! How many girls from our class do you know who actually 'aven't got kids by now?

Danny laughs.

Anthony   It's like if yer 'aven't got a pit bull to parade round yer've gotta 'ave a two-year-old called Chardonnay!

Danny laughs louder.

Anthony   What's that all about?

Danny   Hey, yer shouldn't skit, mate! Bird with a pram . . . it's bound to 'appen to you sooner or later.

Pause.

The kitchen. **Ann***'s mobile starts to ring.*

Ann   That's mine.

She goes into her bag, takes out her mobile.

Kathleen   Who is it?

Ann looks intently at the screen.

Kathleen   Well, are yer gonna answer it?

Ann   Yeah, it's withheld.

She answers.

Hello?

Kathleen *watches her.*

Ann   She's not 'ere, who's this?

Kathleen   Who's . . . ?

Ann   Oh, right. Hang on.

She exits with the phone. **Kathleen** *is confused.*

The turf. **Anthony** *shakes his head, staring into space.*

Anthony   I can't stand the thought of bein' the same as all the others. Workin' a shit, dead end job just to keep a roof over me 'ead. Workin' like a slave all week to trudge down to the same pub, get pissed with the same people, then go an' do it all again week in, week out . . .

Danny   Some people 'ave to.

Anthony   No, they let themselves get trapped, kid. I'm not gonna do it.

Danny   Let themselves get trapped?

Anthony *looks up at him in silence.*

Danny   Even when their 'usband or father fucks off an' leaves them penniless?

Anthony   I . . .

Danny   Even when they've got the chance to get out an' play professional footy but then everythin' goes to shit because they break their leg just before the fuckin' trials?

Anthony *looks his way.*

Anthony   Ee are, I wasn't talkin' about you!

Danny   Don't think I'm some waster just settlin' into me rut, lad.

Anthony   No, I don't, I meant all the others . . .

Danny *takes a long drag of his spliff, shaking his head.*

Danny   This close, mate. You know how close I was to Bolton. Spittin' distance.

Anthony *looks at him in silence.*

Anthony   Where's this come from?

Danny   Fuckin' . . . you! Yer rippin' everythin' to bits!

Anthony   Not you, though.

Danny   I coulda been out'v 'ere now, livin' the fuckin' life on thirty grand a week . . . I 'ad that chance but it fucked up on me . . .

Anthony   I know . . .

Danny   This place was gonna be dust for me. History. Now I'm fuckin' stuck, workin' like a slave . . .

He goes and kicks part of the fencing.

Coverin' the place in this shite to make up for me dad who's disappeared an' me so-called big brother who's a fuck-up in a jail cell!

They are both silent for a moment.

There's nothin' in your way, it's right there . . .

He slides his fingers through the fence.

There's nothin' in the way, yer can touch it, grab it . . . so why are yer 'ummin' an' 'ahin'?

Anthony   I'm not, I'm just . . . I don't know . . .

Danny   I reckon yer do.

Anthony *laughs.*

Danny   Maybe yer've spent too long slummin' it with me an' me ma?

Anthony   I'd never say that about you.

He looks away.

Or Kathleen.

Danny   No, but that's exactly who yer meant, 'cos we are what you're talkin' about. We're livin' our lives 'ere, workin' our balls off to pay the bills, doin' what we need to, lad, it's life!

Anthony   An' what d'yer get out'v it in the end?

Danny   Yer just get on with it, yer don't think about where yer gonna end up.

Anthony   Well, I do. I wanna end up somewhere better than . . .

Danny   Me.

Anthony   It's not about you.

Intense silence. They look at each other.

Danny   You sure about that?

He stares at **Anthony** *as he takes the spliff from him.*

Ann *returns to the kitchen, looking a bit worse for wear.*

Kathleen   Who was it?

Ann   Oh . . . catalogue, bloody chasin' as usual.

Kathleen   What d'yer owe them?

Ann   Oh fuck-all, I paid for it months ago.

Kathleen   Oh aye.

Ann *sits down.* **Kathleen** *watches her.*

Scene Six

Turf. **Danny** *holds the spliff between his lips as he scuffs the ball about beneath his feet.* **Anthony** *watches him, deep in thought for a moment.*

Anthony   Come with me.

Danny *laughs.*

Anthony   What?

Danny   Don't patronise me.

Anthony   Who's patronisin'?

Danny   'Poor Danny's stuck 'ere for life, I'll humour 'im an' invite 'im along.'

Anthony   That shit makin' you paranoid?

Danny   Don't pity me!

Anthony   Is that what you think I'm doing?

Danny   Don't know what to think of you, to be honest.

Anthony   You know me better than that, Danny.

Silence. **Danny** *shrugs and looks down at his feet.*

The kitchen.

Ann   What?

Kathleen   You've gone grey.

Ann   I told yer, I've been a bit iffy all day.

Kathleen   How much is it?

Ann   What?

Kathleen   How much d'yer owe them?

Ann   I told yer, I don't owe them anythin'!

Kathleen   Then why d'yer look like yer've suddenly got the weight of the world on yer back?

Ann   The bloody suspicious mind on you, Kathleen Williams!

Kathleen   Tell me then.

Ann   There's nothin' to . . .

Kathleen   I'd rather 'ave a thief in me kitchen than a liar, Ann!

Ann   I'm no bloody liar! I might be plenty of things but I'm not a liar!

Kathleen   Then go on . . .

Ann   Kath, leave it, will yer?

The turf.

Danny   You think you're the only one?

Anthony *is silent.*

Danny   Are you fuckin' screamin' but the sound doesn't come out yer mouth? Are your knuckles bleedin' from punchin' the walls all day?

Anthony *stands and starts to play with the ball. They are quiet for a moment as* **Anthony** *messes around with the ball.*

Danny   Yer think I've settled for less.

Anthony   I didn't say that.

Danny   Yer say one thing an' mean another! What 'appened to bein' straight?

Anthony   What's that supposed to mean?

Danny   We're not that different, Anthony. Hate to disappoint yer there.

Anthony   Who said we were?

Danny   You did.

Anthony *moves to respond, then stops. Uneasy silence on the turf and in the kitchen.*

Kathleen *watches* **Ann** *smoke.*

Ann   It was the 'ospital, all right?

Silence.

Happy now?

Kathleen *takes a long drag.*

Ann   Fuckin' liar! Me!

Kathleen   Hospital? Who's in 'ospital?

Ann   Me! Tomorrow if they get their own way!

Kathleen   Y'what?

Ann grabs her bag. She dips into it and takes out a letter. She hands it over to her. **Kathleen** *reads it over.*

The turf. **Anthony** *clears his throat.*

Anthony   Imagine the life we'd 'ave.

Danny   Livin' off the fat of the land?

Anthony   Me an' you, lad, out there. Over the fence, over fuckin' St John's Tower an' the Liver Birds . . . over this.

Danny   I don't need to fly 'alf way round the world to know where I'm from. This is me now. If I decide I wanna change, maybe I'll do it. Right now, though, bills to pay an' all that.

He throws the last of the spliff down and stamps on it.

I'm knackered. Gonna get an early night.

He stands and goes to head off. **Anthony** *stands.* **Danny** *turns to him.*

Danny   You comin', then?

Anthony   Don't know.

Danny *looks surprised.*

Anthony   What's the look for?

Danny   You're goin' 'ome to yours?

Anthony   I can do that sometimes, yer know.

Danny *laughs.*

Anthony   Ah, fuck it, yours is closer.

He kicks the ball to **Danny**. **Danny** *picks it up.* **Anthony** *moves to leave, as* **Danny** *starts to kick the ball against the fence.* **Anthony** *folds his arms to stand and watch him for a moment.*

Anthony   Dan.

Danny *starts to kick it more aggressively.*

Anthony   Yo! Ball control!

Danny *kicks it harder until it hits a snag and punctures.* **Anthony** *chuckles.*

Anthony   Ah, now you've done it.

Danny   Cheap piece a' shite.

He exits, leaving **Anthony** *alone.* **Anthony** *goes to the punctured ball, then leaves it.*

The kitchen.

Kathleen   What's this for? Did yer go?

Ann   What?

Kathleen   This! The appointment on the letter! What was it for?

Ann   Me last smear, they found abnormal cells, didn't they?

Kathleen *is quiet.*

Ann   They wanted me back in on Friday.

Kathleen   Did yer go?

Ann *shakes her head.*

Kathleen   Why the bleedin' 'ell not?!

Ann   Oh ee are, if yer just gonna give me the Spanish Inquest I'll be off!

Kathleen   Ann, why didn't yer go?

Ann   I don't know, I panicked, I shit meself.

Kathleen   It could be nothin'!

Ann   Or it could be . . .

They are silent.

Kathleen   Now they're phonin' yer?

Ann I'd rather it was the catalogue. Even the fuckin' Provvy.

Kathleen Ann, if they're phonin' yer, sendin' yer letters . . .

Ann It must be bad.

Kathleen No it mustn't, they might wanna set yer mind at rest.

Ann *laughs.*

Kathleen Don't laugh, Ann.

Ann If I don't laugh, I'll . . . go off me 'ead. They want me in at eleven o'clock tomorrow.

Kathleen An' yer goin'.

Ann Oh, am I?

Kathleen Abnormal cells, they told our Kirby abnormal cells an' she only needed laser treatment!

Ann Yeah, an' they told Sheila Gilfoyle abnormal cells, the poor cunt's six feet under now!

Kathleen *shakes her head.*

Ann I can't, Kathleen.

Kathleen No!

Ann *looks at her.*

Kathleen You will.

Blackout.

Scene Seven

Kitchen. 'Baby Love' by Diana Ross and The Supremes is playing on a tinny CD player as **Ann** *shakes her hips to the music, pouring herself a gin. She is dressed for a night at the bingo. Enter* **Kathleen** *in a bathrobe, carrying an outfit on a hanger.*

Kathleen D'yer reckon this is all right, Ann?

Ann   Oh 'ey, Kath, we're only goin' the friggin' Mecca!

Kathleen   The black one was too tight. Oh 'ey, I'm on a diet as of tomorrow, I'm not turnin' up on Friday lookin' like Fearne Cotton!

Ann   You don't need to bloody diet, he liked you enough to ask you out, didn't he?

Kathleen   There's a big difference when yer've got the right clothes on, Ann!

Ann   Yer plannin' to take them off Friday, then?

Kathleen *lays the outfit across the back of a chair.*

Kathleen   Am I shite! Who was on the phone?

Ann   One'v Danny's mates, I told 'im he still wasn' back from football.

Kathleen   He's had nothin' to eat, the little get.

Ann   I'm sure he'll sort 'imself out, Kath, he's not five years old.

Kathleen   I know.

Ann   Mind you, he acts like it sometimes, the way he talks to you.

Kathleen   He does an awful lot for me as well, Ann.

Ann   Still doesn't give 'im the right to talk to you the way he does sometimes! I mean, who's he to dictate yer life?

Kathleen   That's what they do, though, isn' it? Kids. The minute they arrive, everythin' is about them.

Ann   He's not a kid any more, is he?

They are silent as **Kathleen** *goes about her business.*

Ann   I'm glad I didn't 'ave any kids, yer know.

Kathleen (*getting the ironing-board out*)   Ah 'ey, mine aren't perfect but they're not that bad, girl!

Ann   No, I don't mean that, I mean . . . I'm talkin' about me, I don't think I'd have been able to do the job you've done.

Kathleen *nods, plugging the iron in.*

Ann   I mean me choice a' fellers probably 'ad somethin' to do with that.

Kathleen *laughs.*

Ann   The amount of letters I get from different fuckin' jailbirds, I may as well be in a fuckin' prison pen-pal scheme!

Kathleen   Yeah, I know what yer mean there, don' I?

Ann   Your Chris is a good lad, Kath, just a victim of circumstance.

Kathleen   Yer can say that again. Pour us a drink out, girl.

Ann *goes about making a drink as* **Kathleen** *lays her outfit out on the ironing-board.*

Ann   As for the other feller . . .

Kathleen   Yeah.

Ann *clears her throat. They are both silent for a moment. She hands her the drink.*

Kathleen   That's what's wrong with me sometimes. In town, like with Karl when we've met him, I look at him thinkin' . . . 'Are you another one? Are you gonna promise me the world an' then disappear when me back's turned?'

Ann   Yeah.

Kathleen   Not that the other bastard promised me the world. He *gave* me this.

She looks around. Takes a swig of her drink.

All this was built around 'im, wasn' it? Us. He sorta put 'alf the work in then thought, 'Fuck you, girl, I'm offskies.'

Ann   Kathleen, you're the one who put the work in! You're the one who's seein' it through, not that . . . waste of a ballbag!

Kathleen   No, he was good, Ann. He was good to me, and 'is kids. He was. That's what makes it such a killer.

Ann   How you can call that creature good in any way is beyond me.

Kathleen   Ann, you weren't married to 'im, you don't know how good he was.

Ann   I'm not the marryin' type, am I?

Kathleen   I didn't mean it like that.

Ann   I know, I know. Ignore me.

She sighs. **Kathleen** *laughs and grabs the iron.*

Kathleen   It'll be waterworks in a minute. Change the subject!

Ann (*laughs*)   Well my abnormal cells are always a good laugh.

They burst out laughing.

Kathleen   What a pair.

Ann   Of twats.

They continue to laugh.

Oh, I tell yer what, kid, life's too short, innit? The next time I get chatted up by a pissed student in the Jacaranda I'm takin' 'im 'ome an' . . .

Kathleen   . . . shaggin' 'is brains out.

Ann   Yes, I may as well start livin' up to the reputation!

She pours two more drinks.

Kathleen   Oh, you 'aven't got a reputation!

Ann   Oh yes I 'ave! Accordin' to the local grapevine, I've got a fanny like a wizard's sleeve!

Kathleen *bursts out laughing.*

Kathleen   At least they're givin' some other poor twat a rest.

Ann   My ears'll never get cold in the snow.

Kathleen   Neither'll mine, love.

She swigs her drink. **Ann** *follows suit.*

Ann   Oh, nobody jangles about you.

Kathleen   Who you tryin' to kid?

Ann   Whatta they gonna say?

Kathleen   Oh, take yer pick! Her 'usband pissed off! Her eldest lad's in jail for GBH! Sells knock-off gear out'v 'er back kitchen 'cos all the plazzy gangsters feel sorry for 'er . . .

Ann   Show me one bastard who'd say any of that, Kathleen.

Kathleen   Well, they're not gonna say it to you, are they?

Ann   Damn right they won't. People round 'ere respect you, though. They don't respect me.

She pours another pair of drinks.

Kathleen *swigs another drink. On the CD player, 'I'm Still Waiting' by Diana Ross starts to play.*

Kathleen   Oh, turn it up!

Ann   Ahhh.

She turns it up.

Kathleen *sings along to the opening lines of the song, and is then joined by* **Ann***. Together they sing to the end of the chorus.*

Ann *bursts out laughing as* **Kathleen** *sighs. She turns the sound down a little.* **Ann** *goes to the kitchen table, fiddling with her skirt.* **Kathleen** *stops ironing and looks deep in thought for a moment.*

Kathleen   D'yer know what? Don't know if I can be arsed with the bingo tonight.

Ann   Oh well, thank fuck you said that, these tights 'ave been doin' my 'ead in!

She reaches under her skirt and pulls them down.

Kathleen   Oh 'ey, Ann!

Ann   I know, terrible, isn' it?

She puts them in a pile on the kitchen table.

Kathleen   So we stayin' in, then?

Ann   We are now, the tights are on the table!

Lights fade on the kitchen. Diana Ross plays for a few moments until the lights come back up.

Scene Eight

Kitchen. Diana Ross fades into the background on the small CD player on the kitchen worktop. **Ann** *is raiding the fridge for alcohol until* **Kathleen** *enters. She is carrying* **Danny**'*s goody box.*

Ann   It's been ages since I've done this.

She sparks up and takes a pull. She smiles, sits back.

Kathleen   Nice?

Ann (*exhales*)   Good shit that, kid.

Kathleen *chuckles and takes the spliff from her.*

Kathleen   Jesus.

Ann   Yer all right, kid?

Kathleen   Yeah.

She settles down.

Danny'll kill us.

Ann   Oh, he can try.

Kathleen   Too right, he 'as the 'ouse stinkin' of it some nights, it's about time I 'ad a go.

They fall silent and listen to Diana Ross in the background.

Ann   Doesn' 'alf take me back.

Kathleen   He 'ated Diana Ross. I always played 'er every Sunday afternoon. Or Aretha, take yer pick. He 'ated them.

Ann Pig.

Kathleen I know.

Ann I'm a Patsy Cline girl, as yer know.

Kathleen Oh aye, yeah. Too much of 'er an' yer'll slash yer wrists though, girl. I'm bad enough without listenin' to 'A Church, a Courtroom and Good-fuckin'-bye'.

Ann laughs, takes a pull of the spliff.

Kathleen Yer thinkin' about tomorrow?

Ann Too right I am. I'll be OK, though.

Kathleen Of course yer will. Yer get a gut thing, don't yer? When somethin's wrong? It's gonna be OK.

Ann Yeah. Hundred per cent.

Kathleen takes a pull.

Ann Well. Ninety-eight.

Kathleen What about the other two per cent?

Ann *(laughs)* Patsy Cline, girl. Patsy Cline.

There is silence for a moment.

Kathleen *takes the ashtray and goes to the bin.* **Ann** *sits in silence.*

Ann Kath . . .

Kathleen Yeah?

Ann If I get really bad . . . don't come an' see me in the 'ospital.

Kathleen *turns around swiftly.*

Ann I wouldn't wanna end up like . . .

Kathleen Stop it!

Ann I know.

Kathleen *bangs the ash into the bin, shaking her head. As she does, she glances out of the window.*

Kathleen   Fuck! It's our Danny!

Ann   Shit!

Kathleen   Put that out an' spray yer perfume!

She grabs the stash box and exits. **Ann** *stubs the spliff out and takes her perfume out of her bag, spraying it until the entire kitchen reeks of it. She chuckles to herself as the door opens.*

Anthony *and* **Danny** *enter the kitchen.* **Ann** *and* **Kathleen** *are both increasingly intoxicated.* **Anthony** *looks wound up, like he has a lot on his mind.*

Ann   Hiya, lads!

Danny   Jesus, it smells like a whore's handbag in 'ere!

The lads cough as **Ann** *smiles deliriously.*

Ann   We 'ave to smell nice for the fellers!

Anthony *sniffles suspiciously.* **Kathleen** *enters, looking flustered.*

Kathleen   Danny!

Danny   Mum?

Kathleen   Yer, er . . . all right, lad?

Danny   Er . . . yeah?

Kathleen   Good.

Danny *and* **Anthony** *regard the ladies with confusion.*

Ann   Good game?

Danny   Yeah, it was.

Kathleen   Good.

Ann   Ahh.

Danny   You two bin bevvyin' again?

Ann   Aye, we've 'ad a few.

Danny   Ah 'ey!

Kathleen   We've 'ad a couple 'cos we were goin' the bingo!

Danny   What, yer need to be pissed to go the bingo?

Anthony   Wouldn't you? Have you seen the beauts that go in that Mecca? It's like the Grafton with cash prizes!

Ann   Hey! We go in there an' all, yer know!

Danny   Enough said!

The lads laugh. **Danny** *raids the fridge and brings out two bottles of beer.*

Kathleen   Ee are, yer all right slaggin' us two off for drinkin'!

Danny   I am, yeah.

Anthony *leans against the sink.*

Kathleen   Come an' sit down, lad, come on! I know you appreciate me even if me own son doesn't!

Anthony *smiles, then looks towards* **Danny**, *who frowns as he opens the bottles.*

Kathleen   How is yer mother, Ant?

Anthony *shrugs.*

Ann   Whatta yer askin' 'im for, Kath? He's always bloody 'ere!

Danny   He's not the only one.

Ann *laughs.* **Kathleen** *laughs, shooting a forbidding look towards her son.*

Anthony   She's fine, yeah.

Kathleen   Yer both always welcome in my 'ouse.

Danny   Whatta you on, Mum?

Ann *sniggers.*

Kathleen   So 'ow was footy tonight, then?

Danny   Fine.

Anthony   Yeah, it was . . .

Ann   Like a little Wayne Rooney you, aren't yer, Dan?

Kathleen   Only my Danny doesn't look like Shrek!

*They all laugh, apart from **Danny**.*

Kathleen   Do yer, lad?

Danny nods, rolling his eyes.

Ann   Are you as good as Danny, Ant?

Anthony   Me?

Danny   Or is Danny as good as 'im, yer mean?

Anthony *looks at him apprehensively, then looks away.*

Kathleen   What's that mean?

Anthony   Not'n'.

Danny   Jack shit.

There is a lingering silence.

Ann   Friggin' faces on you two! How old are yers? Yer should be enjoyin' yerselves!

Danny   Like you two?

Kathleen   Hey, we 'ave a friggin' laugh, us!

Ann   You tell 'em, girl.

Danny   Yeah, we know about your laughs, Ann.

Anthony *sniggers.*

Ann   Y' what?

Anthony   Ignore 'im.

Danny   Yeah, ignore me.

Kathleen   Have you two been windin' each other up or somethin'? The pair a' yers are in a bloody weird mood.

Anthony   Na, we've just bin chattin' shit all night.

Danny   No, *you've* been chattin' shit all night, I've bin listenin'.

Anthony *nods, rolls his eyes, takes a swig of his drink.*

Ann   I think you two smoke too much.

She stands and exits the kitchen.

Kathleen   D'you two mind?

Anthony   Eh?

Danny   What?

Kathleen   That girl's got enough on 'er plate.

Anthony   Ee are, I've said nothin'!

Danny   She knows where the door is if she doesn't like it!

Kathleen   Yeah, an' so do bleedin' you!

She pours herself another drink. **Ann** *comes back, about to enter, but stops at the doorway. She listens for a moment.*

Danny   An' what's that supposed to mean, like?

Kathleen   Just wrap up, OK?

Anthony   Ignore 'im, Kath, it's me he's pissed off with.

Danny   D'you wanna stop tellin' people to ignore me?

Anthony   D'you wanna stop tryin' to pick fights?

Kathleen   Oh, yers are like a friggin' married couple! What's goin' on?

Anthony   Danny thinks I'm some sort of snob.

Ann *enters, fixing her skirt.*

Ann   Why's he a snob?

Anthony   Just because I'm gettin' off, that's all.

Kathleen   Gettin' off where?

Anthony *shakes his head.*

Ann   Where yer gettin' off to?

Anthony   Doesn't matter.

Kathleen   Well it obviously does, the face *he's* got on 'im!

Anthony *turns to* **Danny**.

Anthony   An' why's it such a problem that I wanna go?

Danny   Not my problem, kid, you do what yer wanna do!

Anthony   Oh yeah, no problem, like, but yer walk round with yer face trippin' yer abarr it.

Danny   Whatever, kid, think what yer want.

Anthony   Yeah, I think what I want, not what the rest of them do.

Danny   Oh, an' I do?

Kathleen   But where . . .

Anthony (*raising voice*)   Australia, Kathleen! I'm goin' to Australia!

There is silence.

Ann   Bite 'er 'ead off.

Anthony *laughs, looking more and more wound up.*

Kathleen   For an 'oliday?

Anthony   No way.

Kathleen   Emigratin'?

Ann   Like our Ronnie?

Anthony   No. Not like your Ronnie. Not to be some scouser who emigrated to live in a nice 'ouse with a pool.

Ann   Eh?

Anthony   I'm goin' to see it. See the life. See what it's like. Have a go.

Ann   But yer *will* be a scouser, emigratin' . . .

Danny   Ooh, careful, Simmo, yer don't wanna be upsettin' the lad now, callin' 'im a scouser.

Anthony   Piss off, Danny.

Kathleen   Well, that's good, isn' it? If he's goin' off, doin' what he wants to do.

Danny   Yeah, it's great, Mum.

Anthony   Yeah, Danny just thinks because I want somethin' more for meself that I must think less of 'im.

Kathleen   Don't be so daft, Danny!

Danny *guffaws.*

Anthony   Yeah, 'cos it's all well an' good for 'im to stand there an' say it's up to me whether I go or not, but look at 'im! He's fuckin' fumin' that I'm goin' an' makin' somethin' of meself an' he's just stayin' put to be one of the lads.

Danny   An' you're not a snob?

Kathleen   Just 'ang on a minute! What brought this Australia business on, anyway?

Anthony   I'm just sick of this.

Kathleen   What, sick of us?

Anthony *falls silent.*

Anthony   No, not yous.

Danny   That was convincin'.

Kathleen   Do we wreck yer 'ead that much, Ant?

Anthony   You don't, Kathleen.

Ann   Oh, but the rest of us do.

Anthony   No one asked you.

Kathleen   Excuse me, Anthony, this isn't like you.

Ann   Cheek . . .

Anthony   Which?

Kathleen   Talkin' to Ann like that.

Ann   What's wrong with my sister emigratin' to Australia?

Anthony *laughs.*

Ann   What?

Kathleen   Forget it, Ann.

Ann   No, Kathleen, I don't like his attitude tonight.

Anthony   Oh pardon me, *Simmo* of all people doesn't like *my* attitude tonight! Maybe yer can add me to yer list of people yer can't stand, then yer can sit there rippin' me to bits as long as I can't 'ear yer.

Kathleen   Anthony!

Ann   Let 'im say what he wants, Kathleen, I couldn't give a shit.

Kathleen   Well, I do.

Ann   What's wrong with my sister wantin' a new life for 'erself an' 'er kids? How's she any different from you?

Anthony   I said nothin' about your sister!

Kathleen   Now now . . .

Anthony   So I wanna get out there an' do somethin' with me life . . . So I don't wanna sit around this kitchen table smokin' an' drinkin' an' talkin' about the neighbours for the rest a' me life! So I don't wanna spend every Sunday night in the Dead 'ouse listenin' to John Mac singin' 'Vindaloo' on the karaoke! Fuckin' Dead 'ouse, 'as there ever bin a truer name for a pub on fuckin' Mill Street?

Ann   Them places are all we've got round 'ere, remember!

Anthony   I want more than what we've got round 'ere.

Kathleen   We don't do too bad, us!

Ann   We certainly don't, Kathleen, but he seems to think different.

Anthony   That's it. I think different.

Kathleen   Oh, so every bastard should think exactly the same as you do, then?

Anthony   Na, they're all too busy thinkin' the same as each other! One bloody uneducated opinion shared by a coupla thousand people, that's what it is. One straight line runnin' from A to B an' nowhere in between.

Danny *moves to exit.*

Anthony   Every person is the same.

Danny *stops.*

Anthony   Except me.

Kathleen   An' what makes you so different?

Anthony   What makes me . . .

He laughs.

Ann   You laughin' at us?

Anthony   No. I'm not laughin'. I'm not in on the joke that you lot are all in on. You're all ploddin' along, laughin' an' smilin' an' keepin' each other goin' an' I'm . . . I'm standin' underwater an' every time I try to move me legs are like lead an' the water's gettin' in an' I'm . . . drownin'.

Ann   Eh?

Anthony   No one makes fried rice like Chinks!

Ann *frowns.*

Anthony   That right?

Ann   What?

Anthony   Lisa 'ad a chip on 'er shoulder because they all 'ave, 'aven't they, Ann? All them 'alf-castes who don't know whether they're one colour or the other.

Kathleen   Quiet.

Anthony   That lad who cuts Kathleen's 'air, he's comical, isn' he? They all are. Queers. Dead funny. Good for a laugh.

Kathleen   OK, quiet.

Anthony   I'm the only one who winces when you say that shite!

Kathleen   Anthony!

Anthony   What?!

Kathleen   When I say quiet in my kitchen, I want you to be quiet!

Anthony   Don't yer understand what I'm sayin'?

Kathleen   Do *you*?

Ann   He'd be the only fuckin' one.

She sits down with a forced laugh, looking shaken.

Kathleen   You go on about everyone round 'ere bein' the same, but that's not what you mean! You mean you wan' everyone to be the same as you!

Anthony   I don't mean that.

Kathleen   People live this way. People think this way. It's not always your way.

Anthony   It's not about my way!

Kathleen   No. It's not!

Ann   Queer lads *are* funny.

Anthony *sighs and* **Danny** *chuckles.*

Anthony   You still 'ere?

Danny   Too fuckin' right, I'm not missin' this floor show.

Anthony   Floor show's right.

Ann   Yeah, now we're 'earin' it, aren't we? Fuckin' floor show, eh, that's all you think my life is!

Anthony   What do I know about your life?

Ann   Fuck all. You know fuck all an' if you did know 'alf of it you'd be treatin' me with a bit more respect right now, lad.

Anthony   Why should I treat yer with respect when yer don' even treat yerself with any?

Kathleen   Anthony Carter, you watch what you're sayin'.

Anthony   So whose tights are they?

He points to the tights on the table. **Danny** *chuckles.*

Ann   So what? So I'm not one of these women like yer mother . . .

Anthony   My mother?

Ann   Who's lucky enough to find 'erself the right man at the right time. So I'm not the type to settle down an' play 'ouse. Play 'appy families! Tell yer what . . .

She steps up to him.

Maybe *I* want more than what *you've* got.

Anthony *falls silent.*

Ann   All these fuckin' sanctimonious twats who think I'm not good enough . . . who think the way I live isn't good enough . . .

Anthony   Like me?

Ann   Maybe they're not good enough for me. Why are you always here, Anthony?

Silence.

Come on, then! I'm an old slapper. I've got no one but a gang of sisters who live miles away an' wouldn' even trust me to baby-sit. I 'ave to cling to Kathleen because the poor twat's the only person I know who's on more tranquilisers than me!

Danny *looks to his mother with a frown.* **Ann** *grins.*

Ann   So what's your fuckin' excuse, Mr Golden Boy?!

Anthony *is breathing heavily, his eyes filling.*

Ann   You've got a lovely mother, she always lets on. Bit quiet, like, but that's up to 'er. Yer dad's always there to buy us a drink in the Inglenook but never expects anythin' in return. So why can't you stand bein' in your own home?

Kathleen   Ann . . .

Ann   No, Kath, he's had his say, let's 'ave some answers, eh?

Anthony   You offend me, Ann.

Ann *looks confused.*

Anthony   You all offend me. You offend me when you say 'nigger'. You offend me when you say 'Chink'. You offend me when you say 'queer'. You offend me when you let the kids park robbed cars in the driveway. You offend me when you sell knock-off gear out of your kitchen. You offend me when the highlight of your conversation is a bench on Mill Street.

Kathleen   I sell knock-off gear because I'm skint, you cheeky little bastard!

Anthony *sighs.*

Kathleen   I'm left with nothin' but the clothes on my back, my book, my shit job, my son workin' his balls off! An' the cunt who left me – his mates do the only thing they can for me by givin' me that gear to sell. Off that kitchen table. Where you eat your tea nearly every night of the week!

Anthony   I don't want that for my life.

Kathleen   Then you go away and you do better! But don't you ever stand in my kitchen, in my fucking house, an' even think of puttin' me down for how I live. How I survive!

Anthony *turns to* **Danny**, *who stands staring at him without emotion.*

Anthony   That's what I'm talkin' about! This is survivin', it's not livin'.

Ann   Maybe it's not livin' to you, but it is to some!

Anthony   An' what if you get 'it by a bus tomorrow?

Ann *falls silent.* **Kathleen** *becomes anxious.*

Anthony   What if you don't wake up?

Ann   I might not.

Kathleen   Ann . . .

Anthony   Exactly. An' then what? You realise you've been rottin' away with nothin' to yer name but a bingo pen . . . an' it's too late.

Kathleen   It's not. It's never too late.

Anthony   It nearly is for me. If I don't go now I never will. An' I'll give in. An' I'll be like the rest of them.

Kathleen   Then go! Bloody go! But don't think you can slag off good people just because you've got yerself in a twist.

Ann   An' what do you mean by me offendin' yer with the things I say? You're not black or Chinese . . . or . . .

Danny   Queer.

Silence. **Anthony** *and* **Danny** *stare at each other for a moment. A twitching smile spreads across* **Anthony**'*s face.*

Kathleen   Y' what?

Danny   He's a queer. He's a fuckin' queer, Mum.

Kathleen *looks at* **Anthony** *with confusion.* **Ann** *smiles, covers her mouth.*

Kathleen   Are yer, Ant?

Anthony   Me big secret. Danny's rumbled me, Kath. Your son's top of 'is class.

Kathleen   Like, gay?

Anthony   Just like Steven, who's doin' yer caramel layers. Just like the two students who lived in the maisonettes down the street who got their windows put in once a month.

Ann   That's not for bein' poofs, it's 'cos they're grasses.

Anthony   Grasses 'cos they told the bizzies about the robbed cars parked outside their 'ouse!

Kathleen   So that's what this is about?

Anthony   What what's about?

Kathleen   The attitude!

Ann   Gives 'im no right to talk the way he 'as, Kath!

Kathleen   No, it certainly doesn't because d'yer know what, lad?

Anthony   What's that?

Kathleen   You've spent all this time in my 'ome an' yer know nothin' about me or mine.

Danny   No wonder yer were all over that ponce with the pink Mohican before.

Kathleen   Danny.

Danny *chuckles, shakes his head. He turns and exits.* **Anthony** *turns to him just as he leaves. There is silence on* **Danny**'s *exit.* **Anthony** *closes his eyes.*

Anthony   One down.

Ann   Most gay lads I've seen *are* funny. I wasn't bein' nasty when I said that, I meant it.

Anthony's *eyes remain fixed on the doorway where* **Danny** *stood.*

Anthony   I'm not arsed, Ann.

Ann   Well, obviously yer are, the carryin's on outta yer tonight! I mean, plenty a' people 'ave enough to say about me when they know nothin'. Includin' yerself, sunshine! Why would I wanna make someone feel the way I get made to feel?

Kathleen   I think it's about time you took a good long look at yerself, lad, because the things yer say now can stick for a friggin' long time.

Anthony *looks back at them.*

Anthony   What, so yer think I'm not really gay, then?

Kathleen   I couldn't give two shits whether you're Arthur or Martha, I'm talkin' about what you say about others! What you think about others! Looks to me like the problem's in yer own back kitchen, not mine.

Anthony   Everythin's fine in our kitchen.

Kathleen   Then why are yer always in mine?

Anthony *turns away from them.* **Ann** *looks awkward and nervous.*

Kathleen   I think you should go now, Ant.

He looks at her in surprise.

Go on. You've 'ad yer say.

Anthony   Knew this'd 'appen once I told yers.

Kathleen *looks at* **Ann** *with a shake of the head.*

Kathleen   Nothin's 'appenin' that you 'aven't made 'appen!

He is silent.

Anthony!

He looks at her nervously.

Grow up.

Anthony *looks up, a look of realisation on his face.* **Kathleen** *looks disappointed. He looks to* **Ann**, *who grabs her tights and puts them in her bag. He slowly heads for the exit. As he leaves,* **Kathleen** *returns to the table and sits down.*

Ann   Fuck this.

Kathleen   Hey?

Ann   Get them clothes on, we're goin' out.

Kathleen   You're kiddin', aren't yer? Now?

Ann   We're not sittin' 'ere like this, kid, we're goin' out an' livin'!

Kathleen   Ann . . .

Ann   Don't 'Ann' me! I could be about to find out I've got six months to bloody live, kid, I'm not wastin' another minute.

Kathleen   Don't talk like that.

Ann   I'll talk 'ow I want an' so will you! An' these bastards?!

She picks up her tights and carries them to the bin.

Varicose veins be damned!

Kathleen *starts laughing and stands up. She grabs her outfit from the back of the chair.*

Ann   That a girl.

Kathleen   Give me ten minutes.

Ann   Send lover boy a text, see if he's about!

Kathleen   Have you seen the kip of me?

Ann   I don't care, do it!

Kathleen *chuckles and exits in a swoop as* **Ann** *raises her glass in a toast.*

Ann   Go for yer life!

On 'life' the stage is plunged into complete darkness.

Scene Nine

The kitchen is empty. The lights are on but nobody's home. The fencing is edging further into the kitchen set. After a moment the back door opens and **Anthony** *enters. He is slightly drunk. He looks around, then makes his way through to the other door. He exits through this door. After a moment he returns, and sits down at the kitchen table. He takes off his jacket and hangs it on the back of the chair. He taps his hands on the wood, then stands again and goes to the fridge. He opens it, eventually takes out a bottle of water. He takes a swig as* **Danny** *enters.*

Danny   What are you doin' 'ere?

Anthony *turns, startled, spilling some of the water.*

Anthony   Shit.

He wipes the spillage from his top.

I can get off if yer want.

Danny *is unmoved. After a moment* **Anthony** *moves to get his jacket.*

Danny   Pretty good at runnin' away, aren't yer?

Anthony   I shoulda gone 'ome.

Danny   What, to yours?

Anthony *puts the bottle down.*

Danny   Somewhere yer 'aven't insulted everyone under the roof? Somewhere that isn't full of scum like me?

Anthony   I don't think you're scum. I'd never think . . .

He sits down.

Me 'ead's bin battered.

Danny   What d'yer want me to say?

Anthony   Well, either 'Nice one, good for you,' or 'Fuck off away from me, yer dirty shirtlifter!' Pick a side an' go with it!

Danny   Why should I? You don't congratulate me on bein' straight all the time, do yer?

Anthony   Well, I didn't keep it a secret all this time for you to not give a shit!

Danny   What, so you've come out just to see what I say? Why am I so important all of a sudden?

Anthony   You've always been important, it's your opinion I live by!

Danny   You couldn't give a shit about my opinion! Yer too wrapped up in yerself to care about what I think.

Anthony   I was only sayin' what you were thinkin'.

Danny   No, you were sayin' what you think. An' you think I'm . . . *we're* not good enough for yer.

Anthony   No, I don't.

Danny   Yeah, yer do. An' the attitude you 'ad with my mother, I would 'ave put you through that window, mate.

Anthony *looks up at him.*

Anthony   I wish you had.

Danny   Why should I beat the shit outta yer when you're doin' a good enough job of it anyway?

Silence.

It's you that's scum. In your head, it's you.

Silence.

Anthony   You knew.

Danny *nods.*

Anthony   You knew all along.

Danny *sighs, goes to the window, looks out.*

Anthony   You acted . . . the same, but yer knew . . .

Danny   Why would I act differently?

Anthony   I like . . . men. I'm a queer.

He smiles nervously.

Danny   Sounds like you're the one with the problem, not me. You're the one who's ashamed.

Anthony   Wouldn't you be?

Danny   Probably.

Anthony *smiles, sighs.*

Danny   But I'd deal with it instead of takin' it out on people who actually give a shit about me.

Anthony   I'm tryin' to deal with it.

Danny   Find a better way to do it.

He sits down.

Anthony   I didn't mean to disrespect yer mum.

Danny   Tell yer what, if you talk to her like that again, so help me God, you will be launched out that fuckin' window.

Anthony   I'm sorry.

Danny *looks at him curiously.*

Anthony   I'm sorry you're so pissed off.

Danny   No worries, maybe I'll run away to Australia to clear me 'ead.

Anthony *laughs.*

Anthony   It'd be so cool if you were with me.

Danny   Runnin' away's not gonna make the problem go away, though. It's gonna be stuck right there –

*He leans over and touches **Anthony**'s head with his index finger.*

Danny   – the whole time.

Anthony *flicks his hand out of the way.*

Anthony   Who died an' made you a fuckin' expert?

Danny *stands and exits.* **Anthony** *remains seated. He holds his head in his hands.*

Anthony   Jesus . . .

A moment later, **Danny** *returns with his goody box.*

Anthony   They might not be there, though.

Danny   What?

Anthony   All this shit about, y'know, if I go to Australia I still won't be 'appy because I'll still 'ave all me stress an' everythin' . . . I think it's a load of shite. I 'ate bein' 'ere so me 'ead's wrecked. If I'm somewhere else, it won't be. Australia sounds like the kinda place I can be 'appy, so why not go an' find out?

Danny Yer still gonna get dick'eads over there!

Anthony Yeah, but when's the last time you saw a Mardi Gras on Grafton Street?

Danny *laughs.*

Anthony Or the last time you saw a copy of the *Gay Times* on the magazine stand in the Kwikky?

Danny Yer can get it in town.

Anthony Round 'ere, Danny, not town. Round 'ere. Park Road, Milly, Cockburn Street, Grafton Street, this fuckin' estate . . . Imagine what people'd be like . . .

Danny People won't be arsed, they're just gettin' on with it.

Anthony They won't be arsed as long as I keep it to meself.

He reaches out and grabs **Danny***'s hand.*

Danny Ee are!

Anthony Let's go for a walk.

Danny *starts laughing.*

Anthony Come on!

Danny Fuck off!

Anthony Just to go the chippy. Come on, nice pie dinner for the gay boys!

Danny Wouldn' it be a sausage dinner?

They both laugh.

Anthony What if you were my boyfriend? Think about that, what reaction that'd get.

Danny *takes a drag of his spliff.*

Danny If I was your boyfriend . . .

Anthony Yeah!

Danny   If we were shaggin' . . .

They laugh.

Would you still be gettin' off?

The laughter stops. **Anthony** *lets go of his hand.*

Anthony   I don't . . . what d'yer mean?

Danny   Maybe that's what yer need. If yer met someone 'ere . . . yer wouldn't need to run away.

Anthony   What lad am I gonna meet in fuckin' Don One's or Edwards's?

Danny   So start goin' to other places! The Lisbon an' that . . .

Anthony   With who? I take it you're gonna come with me, then?

He stands and goes to the sink, fills his glass again.

Danny   I'm good at the old YMCA, like!

Anthony *bursts out laughing. Silence while* **Danny** *smokes and* **Anthony** *guzzles his drink. He sighs and burps.*

Danny   How masculine.

Anthony   Masculine. That's the name of the game 'ere, isn' it? Footy . . . everythin's footy. Anfield, Goodison, every lad's got a kit and the one's who 'aven't are a bit girly . . . Dads an' lads . . . know whatta mean?

Danny   Yer like footy yerself.

Anthony   It's not about that, I was sayin' that as an example . . . it's that thing where everythin's the same! An' if yer not the same then yer different . . . an' if yer different then yer may as well just curl up an' die . . . The trackies, the trainies, the footy kit, are yer a red, are yer a blue . . .

Danny   OK . . .

Anthony   Every night, the phone goes – 'Are yer comin' the astro with the boys?' Just fuckin' once I'd like to say, 'Na, I'm stayin' in an' watchin' *Footballers Wives* with me mum.'

Danny *bursts out laughing.*

Anthony There yer go.

Danny Lads get brought up on footy 'ere, that's just the way it is. It's big. What else 'ave we got?

Anthony Two footy stadiums and two cathedrals an' not much else . . . Doesn't exactly *scream* Gay Pride.

Danny *starts to build.* **Anthony** *watches him.*

Danny *(teasing)* Gay Pride!

Anthony *laughs.*

Danny Gay.

Anthony Who'da thunk it, eh? I was shittin' meself! I thought it'd change everythin', an' we'd end up weird with each other!

Danny Weird?

Anthony Like yer thinkin' . . . I don't know, I fancied yer or some shit like that.

Danny *starts laughing, taking a pull.*

Danny An' do yer?

Anthony What?

Danny Yer only human, I mean, I'd understand!

Anthony *laughs.*

He joins him and takes the spliff.

I don't want things to change with you.

Danny *steals his drink again.*

Anthony An' yer mum. The way things are 'ere. In this kitchen. I love this fuckin' kitchen, it's the only place I'm sane, I'm normal, I'm not lookin' at the way I walk to make sure it's not a mince!

Danny You've always minced.

Anthony   Outside I'm different! Everyone's got a girlfriend an' a kid, everyone's got everythin' mapped out in this fuckin' . . . factory of a city.

He takes a pull.

Can yer imagine what it's like for me, goin' out with the lads an' all that crap when I've got jack shit in common with them?

Danny   They're out tryin' to pull birds an' you're tryin' to pull . . . cock . . .

Anthony   Yeah. No.

He blushes, hands him the spliff.

Not just that. Everythin'. I'm not interested. I couldn't care less about any of it.

Danny *takes a pull.*

Anthony   I've grown up. They 'aven't.

Danny   And me?

Anthony   Come off it, you grew up quicker than I did.

Danny   'Ad to.

Anthony   Now you're just playin' the game.

Danny   Oh right, am I?

Anthony   Yeah. It's somethin' yer know 'ow to do, so yer doin' it. Goin' to town, coppin' off, chillin' with yer mates, gettin' stoned . . .

Danny   An' you think that's all I'm about?

Beat.

You gonna tell the lads?

Anthony   Fuck!

Danny   They're yer mates.

Anthony *shakes his head.*

Danny   What?

Anthony   They're people who use the word gay for somethin' stupid yer've done. One a' them turns down a tablet an' he's a faggot. Gay is . . . beneath them, Danny. *I'm* beneath them.

Danny   They say 'gay', they don't know what they're talkin' about. I don't know what I'm talkin' about when I say it, yer just say it. That's what yer do. Yer don't think to yerself, 'Oh, I'd better not say that word, me best mate might be a poof.'

Anthony   I know.

Danny   It's just . . . what yer get used to.

Beat.

An' remember . . . yer talkin' about a gang of lads who worship David fuckin' Beckham! A man who paints his nails pink, wears sarongs, an' poses for magazines with his arse in the 'air! Know what I'm sayin'?

Anthony (*laughs*)   Fuckin' superb, that picture. *Arena Homme Plus* . . . I bought that magazine lookin' over me shoulder like it was a porno or something . . .

Danny *laughs, shaking his head.*

Anthony   See? It's weird!

Danny   No, it's not. I'd probably shag David Beckham, lad.

Anthony *chuckles.*

Anthony   OK.

Danny   The lads won't give jack shit, an' the ones who 'ave got a problem, well . . . fuck them. Besides, why worry when you're goin' to Australia?

Anthony *looks down.*

Danny   Sun, sea, surfers . . .

Anthony *chuckles.* **Danny** *laughs too.*

Danny   Hang on a minute!

Anthony   What?

Danny   OK, we've established the fact that you're a ravin' homo . . .

Anthony   Here we go.

Danny   Now I've got a serious question 'ere . . . 'ow did you an' Lisa . . . ?

Anthony   Oh shit.

He laughs, embarrassed.

Danny   What, we can still talk about this shit, can't we? It's not like yer a bird or anythin'.

Anthony *is silent, a grin on his face.*

Danny   Yer not gonna get all moody on me now yer a queer, are yer?

Anthony   Fuck off.

Danny   Ee are . . .

Anthony *laughs.*

Anthony   OK.

Danny   So yer did shag 'er then?

Anthony   Too right, I did!

Danny   So 'ow did yer get it up? Viagra?

Anthony   No, no, I just . . . I always made sure we did it in 'er bed.

Danny   Why?

Anthony   Fuckin' massive Freddie Ljungberg poster over the 'eadboard.

Danny *laughs and groans at the same time.*

Danny   Nice!

Anthony *nods. He takes a pull of the spliff as they are both quiet for a moment.*

Danny   So . . . Ljungberg, yeah?

Anthony   Yeah!

The next sequence of dialogue is played out quickfire-style.

Danny   Ronaldo?

Anthony   Yeah.

Danny   Cole?

Anthony   Oh yeah.

Danny   Beckham?

Anthony   Yeah.

Danny   Gerrard?

Anthony   Yeah.

Danny   Rooney?

Anthony   Fuck off!

They both start laughing.

Be like shaggin' fuckin' Shrek!

Their laughter grows.

Danny   Gay.

Anthony*'s laughter slowly stops.*

Danny   Yer sure, then?

Anthony *looks at him with a shake of the head.*

Danny   What?

Anthony   No one decides to go an' make life that much harder if they're unsure, mate.

Danny   Hey, that shit 'appens. People get mixed up. When I was a kid I thought I fancied Rick Astley!

Anthony *is silent, then bursts out laughing.*

Danny   What?

Anthony   Rick Astley?

Danny   Ee are, I was eight! It only lasted till Bananarama came on!

Anthony *continues to laugh.*

Danny   Fuckin' *Top of the Pops* . . . messes with kids' heads!

Anthony *groans, holds his head in hands.*

Anthony   I'm gay.

Beat.

Danny *stands, cracking his knuckles.*

Anthony   Yer still fumin' with me?

Danny   I'm too tired to give a shit right now.

He yawns.

Anthony   That spliff did the trick.

Danny   You wanna stay?

Anthony   Erm . . . d'yer mind, like?

Danny   Listen, I want yer to stay, all right?

Anthony   Thanks.

He stands and heads for the door. **Danny** *gets a drink and goes back to the table.*

Danny   Hey, maybe I'll get a decent night's sleep when you fuck off to Oz?

Anthony *laughs.*

He turns and looks at him with a grin. **Anthony** *exits to bed.* **Danny** *starts to build, a look of sadness on his face.*

Blackout.

There is a moment's silence, followed by a sudden outburst of drunken laughter. It's **Kathleen** *and* **Ann**. *The stage remains dark as* **Ann**

starts to sing 'I'm Still Waiting' by Diana Ross. There is laughter as
Kathleen *joins her and together they sing the second verse and chorus..*

Silence. A minute later, lights up on the turf.

Scene Ten

More fencing has spread across the turf. The centre is still open but the edges are closing in. The bench now has more graffiti plastered across it.

Ann (*offstage*)   What are you bloody like, Kathleen Williams?

Kathleen *enters, stops.* **Ann** *enters behind her.*

Ann   I've got an early start in the mornin'!

Kathleen   Long as yer don't bottle out again!

Ann   I've said I wouldn't, 'aven' I?

Kathleen *looks around.*

Ann   Kath, I'm not walkin' from 'ere!

Kathleen   Well, yer shoulda stayed in the taxi!

Ann   Whatta yer playin' at?

Kathleen   I wanted to see it, didn' I?

Ann   See what? This?

Kathleen *nods.*

Ann   It's a bench!

Kathleen   It's all bloody phoney, isn't it, Ann?

Ann   Which?

Kathleen   The grass! Looks like somethin' off a Lego set.

Ann   My bloody nipples are like Lego, it's that cold!

Kathleen *goes to the bench and sits. She looks down at the space next to her.*

Kathleen (*reading*)   Debbie loves John. Tar-la.

She laughs.

Ann   Tar-la?

She reads the bench.

It says TLA, yer daft cow!

Kathleen   Hey?

Ann   True Love Always!

Kathleen   They're kiddin' themselves.

She chuckles.

Ann   Fencin's nearly finished.

Kathleen   I know. Our Danny's bin slavin', puttin' this stuff up, an' then yer've got bastard kids tryin' to pull it all back down!

Ann   Why didn't the soft gets put it all up at once?

Kathleen   Council've said they can't. Bit by bit, it's gotta be.

Ann   They must just wanna drag it out, show people what the place should be like . . .

Kathleen   Like danglin' a carrot?

Ann   Exactly. Like we're all just gobshites . . .

Kathleen   As long as we don't get above our station . . .

They are silent.

He asked me to go home with 'im.

She laughs.

Ann   Who?

Kathleen   Karl.

Ann   What, before?

Kathleen   Just then.

Ann   Oh, so why didn't yer?

Kathleen   Do you know how long it's been since a man saw me in the nude?

Ann   Oh, Kath, yer can't let that put yer off, girl!

Kathleen   It's easy for you, you don't know what it's like . . .

Ann   Why do you assume it's easy for me? It's not fuckin' easy, Kath, it's just as 'ard for me to get me kit off! Fuck's sake!

Kathleen   What did I say?

Ann   Sometimes I just . . . I just think you think the same way as every other cunt!

She stands and moves to exit.

I'm gonna go, I'm ditherin'!

Kathleen   Ann Simmo, don't you dare walk off with a cob on!

Ann   I haven't got a cob on! It's been three years since I last took me clothes off for a man, Kath! Three years, but for some reason people still seem to think I'm loose!

Kathleen   So people used to talk, that was a long time ago.

Ann   Mud sticks, Kath!

Kathleen   Fair enough, but stop actin' like I'm throwin' it!

Ann *goes and sits down next to her.*

Ann   I'm sorry, girl.

Kathleen   Yer right, I do need to let meself go.

Ann   I just wanna see yer get yer life back.

Kathleen   I am.

Ann   Are yer?

Kathleen   Yeah, I am. D'yer know what? Goin' out tonight . . . it's the first night in ages when I 'aven't been fuckin' terrified walkin' out the door.

Ann   I know, girl.

Kathleen   No, I mean all the times we go out an' we roll in stinkin' drunk . . . I've been shittin' meself.

Ann   Yeah.

Kathleen   Tonight, though, in the cab, textin' Karl like a gigglin' schoolgirl . . .

Ann   I know, girl.

Kathleen   I do feel so much better about meself.

Ann   So why are you puttin' yerself off goin' home with 'im?

Kathleen   I don't know . . .

Ann   Don't feel guilty, do yer?

Kathleen   Guilty?

Ann   You *are* allowed to get on with yer life.

Kathleen   That's what I'm doin' . . . I've just gotta take me time, girl.

Ann   Don't take too much time, Kath, yer don't know what's around that corner.

Kathleen   Yeah, an' neither do you, writin' yerself off before yer know anythin' definite!

Ann   I'm not, I'm . . . oh, I don't know any more.

She sits back, looking out at the audience. **Kathleen** *does the same. They sit in silence for a moment.*

Ann   Hear that?

Kathleen *nods.*

Ann   Wilson's Mill.

Kathleen   Aye. Not called that any more, though, is it?

Ann   No. What is it called?

Kathleen   Think it's Spillers, isn' it?

Ann   Hmm.

They sit in silence for a while.

They can't leave anythin', can they?

Kathleen   No.

Ann   They 'ave to change it.

Kathleen   Mill's still the same, though, isn' it?

Ann *nods.*

Kathleen   Sounds weird, doesn' it?

Ann   Yeah.

They are silent.

Like it's alive.

Kathleen *nods.*

Kathleen   Yer don't notice it's there till someone mentions it.

Ann   I notice everythin' these days.

Kathleen *sighs.*

Ann   Never 'ad time to listen before . . .

Kathleen   Yeah.

Ann *rubs her foot on the grass as* **Kathleen** *looks at each wall surrounding the turf. The low hum slowly increases.*

Ann   D'yer think Anthony was right, kid?

Kathleen *is staring into space.*

Ann   Kath!

Kathleen   About what?

Ann   About me! Have I made a fool a' myself, Kathleen?

Kathleen   Have you shite, girl, don't start thinkin' like that!

Ann   I can't 'elp it, love, I've been thinkin' about every little thing these last few weeks.

Kathleen   Since the letter.

Ann   Everythin's just dead clear, Kath, like I was walkin' round without me glasses on all that time an' now . . .

Kathleen   Ann, what d'yer . . .

Ann *covers her eyes, shaking her head. Her lip is quivering.*

Kathleen   Oh, Ann!

She reaches out to her, then stops. She puts her hands on her knees.

Ann   If I've got it . . . an' it's bad . . .

Kathleen *screws up her hands.*

Ann   An' if I end up like what Sheila Gilfoyle was like –

Kathleen *looks away, fighting back tears.*

Ann   – layin' stinkin' in some friggin' 'ospital bed, all bloated an' yeller . . . like I'm wearin' a friggin' 'alloween mask . . .

Kathleen   Yer won't, Ann! Yer friggin' won't, d'yer 'ear?

Ann   But if I do . . . what'll I 'ave to show for it? No kids, no feller, even me 'ouse is rented! Just me an' me fuckin' dabber!

Kathleen   You won't be in that 'ospital bed, kid, so don't even think like that! Even if yer were . . . even if worst came to worst . . . *which it won't* –

Ann *laughs, wiping her eyes.*

Kathleen   – you've got a bloody sight more to show than some, girl! You've got yer sisters, all them girls . . .

Ann   Who I 'ardly see . . .

Kathleen   An' 'ang on a minute! Who am I, just some knobhead?

Ann *looks at her with a grin.*

Kathleen   What would I 'ave done without you, kid? I'd be six feet under by now, I'm tellin' yer!

Ann   Don't be daft . . .

Kathleen   I'd 'ave put a gun to me 'ead if you hadn't been there, Simmo.

Pause.

Ann   I know I said I'm glad I didn' 'ave kids . . . an' I am. But sometimes I wish, sometimes I just wish someone was there, Kath. When I get 'ome. I wish it wasn't just me.

Kathleen   But it's not, girl. An' my home's your home as well, remember.

Ann   No, it's not, babe. I know you try to make me as welcome as possible but that lad was right. I'm a floor show, me, the entertainment.

Kathleen   That lad's confused an' pissed an' stoned, don't be listenin' to 'im, Ann. An' he's in my 'ouse just as much as you are, so he's got no right to talk to you like that!

Ann   He 'as. I shouldn't be imposin' meself on people like this.

Kathleen   Yer not.

Ann *falls silent. She looks at* **Kathleen** *with a shake of the head.*

Ann   Kath. I'm fifty years of age. What am I playin' at, eh?

Kathleen   Whatever it is, keep playin' it, girl. I'd be lost if yer didn't.

Ann   Maybe Anthony's got the right idea.

Kathleen   Doesn't bloody sound like it, the little bastard!

Ann   I mean goin'. I've got our Ronnie over in Australia, remember. Maybe that's what I need to do. Cut me losses an' get out there.

Kathleen   An' what would I do then?

Ann   Yer don't need me, love, yer've got Karl now!

Kathleen   What? Do you think I'd fuck you off for a feller?

Ann   I wouldn't blame yer.

Kathleen   Be'ave yerself, Ann, we're for keeps me an' you.

She shakes her head.

Ann   Don't bank on it, love.

Kathleen   It's gonna be fine. It's gonna be good news.

Ann   Yeah.

She looks around and laughs.

Hey, if it *is* gonna be bad news, I'd rather see it out on a fuckin' beach in Australia than . . .

She looks down at the turf. She runs her hand along the bench.

Even if I *wanted* to die on a bench in the middle of Mill Street . . . the bastards are fencin' it up.

Kathleen   Yer not gonna die anywhere for a good few years, yer daft cow. Yer'll see the day of all of us, you.

Ann   Not you, kid.

Kathleen *chuckles.* **Ann** *is silent. She looks up at the stars.*

Kathleen   Would yer 'ave to be dyin' to go to Australia?

Ann *shakes her head.*

Ann   Be scary, though, wouldn' it? I wouldn't know anyone.

Kathleen   Yer'd know your Ronnie. That's all yer need, innit?

Ann *nods.*

Kathleen   I could visit. Top up me tan.

Ann   The heat out there'd be glorious.

Kathleen   Like when we went to Marmaris last year.

Ann   Oh, that was roastin'.

Kathleen   How would you know? Yer spent most of it indoors with the air-conditionin'!

Ann   But that heat was ridiculous! I only 'ad to blink an' I'd 'ave to change me knickers! When I wore them, ha!

Kathleen *groans and laughs.*

Ann   I'll probably stay put. See me days out in the friggin' Mecca!

Kathleen *chuckles.*

Ann   I want bagpipes, by the way.

Kathleen   Come again?

Ann   At the funeral.

Kathleen   Oh, Ann, what did I just say!

Ann   Listen, *if* it happens! I'm sayin' '*if*'! I want a piper. An' I want 'im to play 'Walkin' After Midnight', OK?

Kathleen   Fuck off.

Ann   D'yer 'ear me?

Kathleen   Yes!

She sighs, closes her eyes. **Ann** *looks at her with a smile. She grabs her hand.*

Ann   I'm only sayin' *if*.

They are silent again. **Kathleen** *takes a couple of deep breaths as* **Ann** *looks more peaceful and content. After a moment* **Kathleen** *gives a musing hum.*

Ann   What?

Kathleen   Where've they moved the bagwash to?

Ann *shrugs.*

Kathleen   Never used it anyway.

Ann   It was a great deal more use than this is.

She knocks on the bench.

D'yer wish yer'd gone 'ome with 'im now?

Kathleen (*smiles*)   He'll keep. He came out last minute just 'cos I texted him. He must be keen!

Ann *laughs.*

Ann   That's me girl.

Kathleen *stands.* **Ann** *follows.*

Ann   Soon as I get the all-clear I'm out there on the sniff.

Kathleen   I'll see if Karl's got any mates – any requirements?

Ann *laughs.*

Ann   A fuckin' pulse!

They chuckle as they exit. Lights up on the kitchen.

Scene Eleven

Kitchen. **Danny** *is sitting at the table, toking on a spliff and staring up at the ceiling. After a moment of silence the door opens and a laughing* **Ann** *and* **Kathleen** *enter.* **Danny** *snaps out of it and sits forward.*

Ann   Aye aye, on the old wacky baccy, ey!

Danny   Jesus, you two look like you've bin in the Pleasure Rooms all night.

Kathleen   We ended up walkin' 'alf the way 'ome. What are you doin', smokin' that in my kitchen?

Danny   I pay just as many bills as you do, I can smoke it where I like.

Kathleen   Oh, can yer now?!

Ann   Hang on! Before round two starts, let me just . . .

She runs to the sink and fills a glass with water. **Kathleen** *walks towards* **Danny**, *who is unmoved.*

Kathleen   Cocky little get, aren't yer?

Danny   Wonder where I get it from.

Kathleen *reaches out and snatches the spliff off him.*

Danny   What are yer playin' at?!

Ann *turns to see* **Kathleen** *put the spliff between her lips and take a pull.* **Danny** *is in shock.*

Ann   Oh, nice one, kid!

Danny   Oh my *God.*

He covers his face.

Kathleen   Sweeeet.

Ann   I'll leave yers to it.

She chuckles as she exits.

Kathleen *sits down at the table, throws her feet up on the chair and takes another pull.*

Danny   Give us it back.

Kathleen   Or what?

After a moment he reaches out, snatches it away and stubs it out.

Danny   What makes you think it's OK to smoke weed in front of me?

Kathleen *laughs.*

Danny   What?

Kathleen   I am your mother and you are sitting in my kitchen smoking it in front of *me*! This is my house, Danny, my house, and you show me no respect!

Danny   It's meant to be our house!

Kathleen   What?

Danny   Me an' you! I'm not the kid any more!

Kathleen   So why be'ave like a spoiled brat?

Danny   I don't!

Kathleen   Yes, you do! The way you talk to me is like you hate me! An' yer hate my friends!

Danny   Her?!

Kathleen   What gives you the right to talk to people like that?

Danny   It's like you've forgot! You've forgot I'm even 'ere!

Kathleen   That's a load of shite, I do everythin' for you!

Danny   I hate it!

Kathleen *stops what she's doing.*

Danny   I hate it, Mum, I hate it!

He tries to fight back tears, clenches a fist and punches the door frame.

Kathleen   Danny!

Danny   I hate him. I wanna kill him, Mum, I wanna find him and kill him!

Kathleen   Danny, what . . .

She immediately goes to comfort him, but he pushes her away.

Danny   Stay away from me.

Kathleen   Danny, stop it.

Danny   I can't! I can't!

Kathleen   Danny!

He butts the door.

Danny, stop it, you'll hurt yerself!

He butts it harder.

STOP IT!

He stops.

Why do you hate me, what have I done?

Danny   You weren't good enough to keep 'im.

Kathleen *covers her mouth.*

Danny   You! You fuckin' . . .

He barges past her to the back door.

Kathleen   Danny!

Danny   Leave me alone!

He opens the door.

Kathleen   You're not dressed, stay put!

He stops, turns to look at her.

Danny, I was a bloody good wife and I did all I could to keep a happy home.

Danny   I feel like I can't stop screamin', I don't know what to do! Why won't yer . . .

Grunts.

Kathleen   What d'yer want me to say?

Danny   I want you to fix it!

Kathleen   It's not my fault he went!

She stops, looks down at her hands and rubs them together.

It's not . . . my fault.

She looks back up at him.

Danny   So it's mine?

Kathleen   No. He went because of his own fault, not ours.

Danny   You think it's my fuckin' fault!

Kathleen   Danny, will you listen to me?

She goes to him.

You're a good lad!

Danny   Why are yer lyin'?

Kathleen *is silent.*

Danny There's fuckin' nothin' good about me! Otherwise he'd have stayed, I woulda bin too good to leave!

Kathleen You are too good to leave, but . . .

Danny Why's he goin', then?

Kathleen What?

Danny Nobody wants to stay with me, Mum.

Kathleen You mean Anthony?

She grabs him by the neck and drags him into her as he cries.

Danny I don't know what to do, I hate it.

Kathleen I know, lad, I know.

Danny It's me.

Kathleen No, no.

She strokes his head, then looks him in the eye.

Listen.

She shakes him.

Listen.

He is silent. He looks down at his feet.

Look at me, Danny!

He looks up.

Y'know what? I'm so proud of you.

Danny I . . .

Kathleen No. You are my son and I'm proud of yer. My lad. Mine.

Danny *dries his eyes.*

Danny Ah, fuck's sake.

Kathleen People leave because of what's in their 'eads, no other reason than that. That's why that lad up my stairs wants to go, that's why your dad went. Not my fault. Not yours.

Danny   OK.

Kathleen   An' yer can call me for everythin' an' yer can say yer hate me, but I'll never leave.

She walks away to continue making her cup of tea. **Danny** *stands there and watches her. He sniffles.*

Kathleen   I don't know what else I can say, Danny.

Danny   Are you gonna see that feller again?

She stops, turns to look at him.

Kathleen   Is that what this is all about?

Danny   Are yer?

Kathleen   Yeah. I'm goin' out with 'im on Friday.

Danny *nods.*

Kathleen   What d'yer think, then?

Danny *collects his goody box together.*

Danny   He'd better be all right.

Kathleen *smiles.*

Kathleen   D'yer wanna cup?

Danny   Na, I'm gonna go to bed.

He makes his way to the door.

Mum, if he's not, leave him. Don't let him leave you.

He exits. **Kathleen** *looks up with tears brimming in her eyes.*

Blackout.

Scene Twelve

Kitchen. **Ann** *is up and about. In last night's clothes, her face pale, she looks quite rough. She is making herself a glass of orange juice. After a moment,* **Anthony** *enters, looking just as wrecked.*

Anthony   Oh . . .

Ann *turns around.*

Anthony *is carrying his shoes. He places them under the kitchen table.*

Ann   D'yer wanna cuppa tea, lad?

Anthony *is tentative. She turns to look at him.*

Ann   Well?

Anthony   Go on, yeah.

She smiles, fills the kettle.

Ann . . .

Ann   What's that?

Anthony   I didn't mean . . .

Ann   I know.

Anthony   I mean, me 'ead was wrecked.

Ann   Meet yer mate.

Anthony   Yer don' 'ate me, then?

She chuckles.

Ann   D'yer wanna piece of toast?

Anthony   What's goin' on?

Ann   What d'yer mean?

Anthony   I called you for everythin' last night an' yer wanna know if I want toast! Why?

She takes bread out and sets up the toaster.

Ann   That's what we do, isn' it? We look after the lads. Yer'll never learn to fend for yerself that way, of course, but . . . maybe that's the point.

Beat.

I was gonna 'ave tea an' toast meself, but I don't think I could keep anythin' down right now.

Anthony   You sufferin'?

Ann *looks at him and nods.*

Anthony   Why don't yer go back to bed?

Ann   Can't sleep, lad.

Anthony   No. Me neither.

Silence as he watches her.

Somethin's up.

Ann   Do you love Danny?

Anthony *looks at her in surprise.*

Ann   Sorry.

Anthony   I . . . yeah. I mean, of course, he's me best mate.

She smiles.

You love Kathleen, don't yer?

Silence.

She grabs him and hugs him. The hug lingers for a moment and then she leaves via the back door. He sits motionless for a bit.

Kathleen *enters in her dressing-gown, looking pretty dire.* **Anthony** *is sitting in silence.*

Anthony   Mornin'.

She stops and looks at him in surprise.

Kathleen   Oh. Mornin'.

She goes to the kettle. There is a very uneasy silence.

I thought I 'eard Ann. Where's Ann?

Anthony   She just left, she's got . . . I think somethin's up.

Kathleen *nods.*

Anthony   Wanna cuppa tea?

He smiles, then stops himself.

Kettle's on, she was just makin' me one . . .

Kathleen *gets another cup out, slams it down. He stands.*

Anthony   Wanna 'and?

Kathleen   No, thanks.

He scratches his head, then takes a few steps forward.

Anthony   Kath?

Kathleen   What?

Anthony   Can I just . . . say somethin'?

Kathleen   Oh, don't let me stop yer, lad.

Anthony   No, it's just . . .

He groans. She turns and looks at him. He smiles sheepishly.

It's mad the way yer can 'ave somethin' arranged in yer 'ead an' then when it comes down to it, everythin' just goes to shit. I shoulda wrote cue cards . . .

Kathleen *is unmoved.*

Anthony   I'm just, like, sorry. For everythin' I said.

Kathleen   Why?

Anthony *looks confused.*

Anthony   What?

Kathleen   If yer meant what yer said then why apologise for it?

Anthony   I didn't, it all sorta came out wrong. I 'ave ten different ways of sayin' things in me 'ead but then when I go to actually say them it comes out . . . a bit like this, really.

Kathleen   What is it yer've got to say? I know yer 'ate bein' 'ere. I know yer gay. I know about yer goin' away. It's not even any a' my business – I'm not yer mother.

Anthony   I wish yer were.

Kathleen *is silent. Beat.*

Kathleen   Don't be stupid! There's nothin' wrong with your mam an' dad.

Anthony   There'll be plenty wrong once I tell them, won't there?

Kathleen   What?

Anthony   They're gonna flip.

Kathleen *lets the kettle reach boiling point.*

Kathleen   Your mam an' dad aren't the flippin' type, lad.

Anthony   You don't know them.

Kathleen   Listen, I know them well enough to know they're not bloody monsters. I grew up with them, remember. We all grew up together.

Anthony   Yeah.

Kathleen   How do you think they'll feel if you do a disappearin' act without ever tellin' them the truth about yerself?

Anthony   Why do they 'ave to even know?

Kathleen   You're their lad. (*Silence.*) And you're planning to fuck off and leave them. When?

Anthony *sighs. He looks up at her.*

Anthony   I've gotta tell the feller today.

Kathleen   Well, yer cuttin' it pretty fine, aren't yer?!

Anthony   It's only nine o'clock!

Kathleen   Tell them. Tell them before you tell any feller you're goin' anywhere.

Anthony   I can't!

Kathleen   Don't be so bloody wet!

Anthony *laughs.*

Kathleen   I'm not friggin' laughin', sunshine! What was that I saw last night?

Anthony   Ah, I know, listen . . .

Kathleen   Get some of that barefaced cheek back about yerself an' you tell them what's what! They need to know.

Anthony   Would you wanna know?

Kathleen *is silent.*

Anthony   I mean . . . if it was Danny, would you wanna know?

Kathleen   Too fuckin' right, lad. I've been kept in the dark before, it's not nice.

Anthony *nods.*

Kathleen   Is he?

Anthony *laughs, shakes his head.*

Kathleen   Well, I 'ad to ask!

I'll be the first to admit it, this place has gone to shit these last few years. Strange faces everywhere, every bastard peddlin' drugs . . . But d'yer know . . . there's still a lot'v good people round 'ere, Anthony. Like your mam an' dad. Good people who turned out in their 'undreds to my mam's funeral. Good people who drop gear off for me to sell to 'elp pay me mortgage. Good people who are good friends who wouldn' 'ave a bad word said about yer.

Anthony   Yeah, good people if yer in with them all, but what if yer not? What if yer the only black kid on the estate? What if yer the only queer kid in the class?

Kathleen   An' yer think that's somethin' to do with the area? Ant, I mean, I might be some hick who's never gone further than Talacre, but I know for a fact you're gonna get bastards wherever you go!

Anthony   You're not a hick.

Kathleen   Anthony, I don't think you're seein' the full picture, lad. People 'round 'ere, they fight.

Anthony   Don't I know it.

Kathleen   No, they fight to get whatever they can. They do what they can. Sell knock-off gear. Graft. Work on the side. But things aren't black an' white, are they?

Anthony   I know.

Kathleen   If things were black an' white I'd be workin' on the side to screw the state an' take taxpayers' money. In colour, Ant, I'm workin' on the side because I am on the bones of my arse. Most people are. D'yer see any bastard throwin' us a bone?

Anthony   No.

Kathleen   No, they threw us a bench. Then they said, 'Oh no, yer can't even 'ave that, yer can look at it through this nice bit of corrugated iron. That you have to put up.'

She goes to the sink and looks out of the window.

Ann reckons they're gonna move that Chinatown arch across the middle of the road, then block it off so we can't get through.

Anthony *bursts out laughing.*

Kathleen   Can yer imagine?

She chuckles too.

Keep the scum outta sight. Urban Splash, Beatles Museum and the Lambanana, that's what we need for 2008. Not scousers.

She looks at him with a straight face.

Not me.

Anthony Or me.

Kathleen Oh, but you won't be 'ere, will yer? You'll be off then, livin' the life. Away from us.

Anthony I don't wanna be away from yous.

Kathleen Think about that before you tar us with the same brush in future.

He is silent. She moves to the kettle.

Anthony Kath, is Ann OK?

Kathleen I don't know, lad.

Anthony What d'yer mean? What . . . don't yer know?

Kathleen What the results'll say.

Anthony *is silent.* **Kathleen** *looks at him and shakes her head. The kettle boils.*

Anthony I'll make the tea.

Kathleen Will yer shite!

Anthony Just sit down!

He goes to the kettle, nudges her out the way. She laughs, goes to sit.

Kathleen One sugar.

Anthony I know, I know!

She smiles and sits. **Danny** *enters, half-asleep.*

Danny Yous are a corny pair a' twats!

Anthony *laughs with a start at his entrance.*

Kathleen Who rattled your cage, Pleasant Hole?

Danny   The fuckin' love-in goin' on down 'ere.

He opens the fridge, takes out a bottle of water, slams it shut and exits again swiftly.

Scene Thirteen

Sunshine is beating down on the turf. **Danny** *is there, erecting fencing to close it off once and for all. In the kitchen,* **Kathleen** *is sitting at the table reading the obituaries in the* Echo. *She is tutting and shaking her head as she reads.* **Danny** *wipes his brow and sits for a moment. He looks at his hands and sits back for a moment.*

Anthony (*offstage*)   Now then

He enters, an STA Travel bag in hand.

Danny   All right, lad.

Anthony   Fuck, so it's nearly done then, eh?

Danny *nods.* **Anthony** *approaches him and* **Danny** *kicks the bag.*

Danny   I could say the same thing to you.

Anthony *laughs.*

Danny   All sorted?

Anthony   Nearly. Got a good rate on the insurance!

Danny   Yeah?

Anthony *sits down next to him.*

Danny   You playin' tonight?

Anthony   Yeah, too right.

Danny   The boys wanna go the Inglenook after it, don't know if yer fancy it?

Anthony   I might do, yeah.

Danny   You comin' to ours for yer tea?

Anthony   Yeah, I was gonna show yer ma some of this stuff.

He shakes the bag.

Danny   Don't be givin' 'er ideas.

Anthony   As if.

Danny *laughs.*

Anthony   You fucked?

Danny   Yeah. It's clearin' me 'ead, though. She went on again at me this mornin' about that VO from Chris.

Anthony   When's it for?

Danny   Saturday. Fuckin' does me 'ead in, seein' 'im, y'know.

Anthony   I'm not surprised.

Danny *shrugs, takes a swig of his drink.*

Anthony   Saturday?

He nods.

Can I come with yer?

Danny   You wanna come an' see our Chris with me?

Anthony *nods.* **Danny** *smiles, takes another swig.*

Danny   Nice one, yeah. In fact . . .

He gets his mobile out.

I'm gonna tell 'er that right this minute to shut 'er up.

He dials a number and the phone next to **Kathleen** *starts ringing. It barely rings once before she snatches it up.*

Kathleen   Ann?

Danny   Bloody 'ell, Mother, let it ring next time.

Kathleen   Oh 'iya, lad, what's up?

Danny   Nothin', just to let yer know we're goin' to see our Chris on Saturday.

Kathleen   Oh lovely, he'll be made up. Who's we?

Danny   Anthony's comin'.

Kathleen   Is he? Oh, good. Hey, listen, d'yer remember Mrs Mac from Elswick Street? Had the shop?

Danny   Think so, why?

Kathleen   Poor cunt's dead.

Danny *laughs.*

Kathleen   Whatta you laughin' at?

Danny   You readin' them deaths again?

Kathleen   It says 'Lovin' son Davie'. Didn't she 'ave two sons?

Danny   I can't remember

Kathleen   They always said the other one was on the gear. Bet yer they've snubbed 'im. Not on, that, is it, lad? I mean, a smack'ead's a smack'ead but it's still the poor woman's son.

Danny   Whatever, Mum.

Kathleen   Unless he's the one who screwed the shop.

Danny   Bit morbid, that, Mum!

Kathleen   Says 'ere she 'fell asleep'.

She chuckles, as does he.

Hope she did more than that or they'll be buryin' the poor cunt alive!

He laughs louder.

I'd better get off the line, I'm waitin' for Ann to ring.

Danny   What's new!

Kathleen   Shut it. See yer later.

Danny   Ta-ra.

They both hang up. He turns to **Anthony**.

The front door slams and **Kathleen** *leaps to her feet. The following exchanges cut swiftly between the turf and the kitchen.*

Danny   Deaths.

Kathleen   Ann?

Silence. **Anthony** *takes the drink from* **Danny** *and swigs as* **Ann** *enters the kitchen. She is smiling in a fragile manner.*

Danny   Well?

Ann   Put the kettle on, Kath.

Danny *stands and goes to the fence.* **Anthony** *remains seated.*

Kathleen   What? What's been said, girl?

Ann *shakes her head, smiling, goes to sit down.*

Kathleen   Ann!

Ann   Just do us a cuppa tea, eh, girl. Will yer?

Kathleen *nods. She goes to the kettle.* **Danny** *turns to* **Anthony**.

Danny   You'd better budge before I trap yer.

Anthony *laughs. He snatches up some of the blades of grass and puts them in his pocket.*

Ann   Oh 'ey, what's this?

Kathleen   Oh, sorry. Are you . . . ?

Ann   Ah, poor Mrs Mac.

Kathleen   Ann . . .

Ann   One of her lads was on smack!

Kathleen   I thought so!

Ann   He was a horror! Didn' 'ave a tooth in 'is 'ead. He died not so long ago.

Anthony   What time you finishin'?

Danny   I'm gettin' off soon as this is up.

Kathleen   My 'ands are shakin'. He died?

Ann   That's why 'is name's not in.

Anthony   Want me to wait?

Danny   Time waits for no man.

They laugh.

Anthony   Weapon.

Kathleen   I thought they'd snubbed 'im.

Ann   Wouln't blame them, he was vile.

Kathleen *laughs.*

Ann   Friggin' 'ell, girl, did you just laugh or was it a ball of wind?

Kathleen   Fuck off, Simmo!

Ann   Speakin' of wind, my stomach feels like me throat's bin cut! Fancy a little banquet?

Anthony   I'm gonna head over then.

Kathleen   Oh, too right I do!

Ann   Get on the blower.

Kathleen   Our Danny's up on Milly, I'll get 'im to call in the Shanghai on 'is way 'ome.

She grabs the phone and dials. **Danny**'*s phone rings.*

Ann   Get us the duck, girl. I feel like duck.

Kathleen   I'll get a proper half, with pancakes.

Danny   Hello? You stalkin' me or somethin'?

Kathleen   What time are you comin' in, lad?

Danny   Barr 'alf an' 'our, why?

Kathleen   Fancy callin' into the Shanghai on yer way?

Danny   Oh, for a change! What for?

Kathleen   Have yer got a pen?

Danny   I'm in the middle of puttin' a fence up, Mum, what do you think?

Kathleen   Well, will yer remember?

Danny   Just get it delivered!

Ann   Is he givin' you grief?

Danny   Oh, tell yer what . . . Ant . . .

Anthony   What?

Danny   Wanna go the chippy for me ma?

Anthony   OK.

Kathleen   Put 'im on.

Danny *hands him the phone, laughing.*

Anthony   Hiya, Kath.

Kathleen   Hiya, love.

Ann   Just phone the order through to the chippy an' get the moanin' twat to pick it up!

Kathleen   Oh.

Anthony   What d'yer want?

Kathleen   I'll phone the chippy, Ant, d'yer mind pickin' it up on yer way over?

Anthony   No, no worries.

Kathleen   All right, I'll give yer the money when yer get 'ere.

Anthony   Yeah, cool.

Kathleen   Tell the other ray of sunshine I'll save 'im some.

Anthony *laughs.*

Kathleen   Ta-ra.

Anthony   See yer.

He hangs up.

Want anythin' from the chippy?

Danny   Na.

Ann   He's a lovely lad. Anthony.

Kathleen   They both are.

Danny   Ant.

Anthony *stops, turns to look at him. Silence.*

Danny   You're goin', aren't yer?

Anthony   Erm . . . yeah. Why?

Danny *looks down, then looks up at him.*

Danny   Just makin' sure. See yer in a bit.

Anthony   Later.

Danny *watches him as he goes. He starts to erect the last piece of fencing. Over the next conversation* **Danny** *is finishing off the fencing, leaving the turf completely blocked off.*

Ann   He robbed them blind, that lad.

Kathleen   Hmm?

Ann   Mrs Mac, the smackhead son.

Kathleen   An' then he pissed off, I knew I was right.

Ann   Poor arl cunt, she never 'ad much luck.

Kathleen *walks over to her with her drink.*

Kathleen   Remember her shop?

Ann   Yeah. Stunk like a wet alley.

The pair of them chuckle. **Kathleen** *watches her as she reads.* **Ann** *eventually looks up, smile on her face.*

Ann   I wonder what they'll say about me.

Kathleen *stops what she's doing.* **Ann** *continues reading.*

Danny *picks up his belongings and leaves the turf.*

Lights down.